CW00504361

There is a Way

The Reiki Revolution

Torsten A. Lange

TORSTEN A. LANGE

There is a Way

THE REIKI REVOLUTION

Creating a New Humanity
and a New Humankind Together

ReikiScience Publications

London | Los Angeles

A world revolution

based on a complementary therapy?

Well, yes!

Because, firstly,

Reiki isn't only a complementary therapy.

It's a door-opener to higher levels of universal energy.

And secondly,

because all other paths have failed.

Contents

Part 2: THE INNER REVOLUTION

1. Realisation

2. Change

3. Application

Part 3: THE OUTER REVOLUTION

There is a Way

Before we start...

Please sit down for a moment, close your eyes, and place your hands on your heart, one hand on top of the other. Try to feel a connection with your heart, then ask yourself:

What needs to change in my life for me to be happier?

Now, listen inside and allow your heart to take you there.

You may see a variety of images, one after the other. Go on an inner journey and create a new life that would make you happy and fulfilled.

Take a moment to let this resonate deeply in your heart.

Now, go one step further and ask again:

How would the world need to change to be a place where everyone could be happy and live together in harmony?

Again, let your heart take you there; create this beautiful utopia, and sense the happiness and peace.

Then move your hands away from your heart, gently open your eyes and slowly come back to reality.

Of course, you'll be aware that this was just an excursion into a fantasy land. But what if we could make it a reality? What if happiness became our everyday experience?

**If we can create a better world in our hearts,
we can create it in reality.**

There is a way
... to enjoy every single day
... to feel deep inner peace
... to bring more meaning into our lives.

There is a way
... to share without losing out
... to have success without it being at someone else's
expense
... to be accepted even though we may be different.

There is a way
... to be free of guilt and shame
... to find understanding and forgiveness
... to live in peace with people we have seen as
threatening.

There is a way to replace fear with love
And to re-connect with our soul.

It's a way that everyone can walk. But we need to do it
together.

Thank you for joining us.

Part I

WHY?

There is a Way – The Reiki Revolution

1.

Why We Need a Revolution

A. THE WORLD AS IT IS

It all begins with love. Or, rather, the lack of it.

Observing what's happening around us, or turning on the news, it's clear to see: There's a distinct lack of love in the world. We see an abundance of fear, anger, violence, oppression, and various other attempts at distracting ourselves in the short-term. But love?

Looking at what's going on in the world keeps our attention from ourselves because, when we're honest, doesn't what's happening in the outside world make our own life look better?

Let's go into a bit more detail – after all, without proper analysis, it's hard to find a solution.

Are YOU in love at present?

Do you love a special someone? Your family? Your friends?

Do you love your colleagues?

Yourself?

Do you love your life? Your job? Your age?

Do you love your soul?

If you took a moment of deep honesty (and you can, because no one else can hear the answer), would you be able to say that love is the dominant force in your life?

If the answer is "yes" (and you are one of the tiny percentage of the population who I assume would give this answer), is this love noticeable by people around you? Are you truly happy?

If so, you'll very likely still find aspects of this manifesto helpful, but you may not really need it. You're already on the path to making the world a better place.

If you're not sure about the answer you feel inside (and who really wants to admit that love is missing from their life?), or the answer is a heartfelt and slightly sad "no", you belong to the overwhelming majority. A lack of love is completely mainstream, just as it is to not be happy.

How did we come to accept so little love in our lives?

It's simple: We see love as the exception rather than the norm. We restrict it to a small circle of people around us, occasionally including a pet, or a hobby.

The rest is just... normal life. After all, you cannot love everyone; we're just too different. And, besides, the demands of our daily lives don't really allow for too much love. We're too busy surviving! We have deadlines, we need to get a job finished, and that's stressful enough – often to a point where we can hardly cope. Otherwise, our competitors overtake us. We are out. We lose our security, our stability. There is no time to be sentimental.

This has happened to us before: The toy that our best friend destroyed when we were five years old; the sibling who seemed to be our parents' favourite; the teacher who constantly overlooked us; the bullying at school that no one noticed. And what about our romantic feelings for some beautiful person when we were sixteen, who didn't care the slightest about our advances?

Often, we feel singled out. And maybe there's a reason. Maybe we're just not good enough; didn't we struggle more at certain subjects than others? Why were we so rubbish at sports? Why did the "cool" factor completely bypass us, especially as our single parent didn't have enough money to buy us the latest fashions that our friends had?

Then, there was the time when we just snapped. Made our best friend feel awful, said something we immediately regretted. And still do. Because there was never a right moment to say "sorry". We feel embarrassment, we feel shame, we feel guilt, but we need to pretend we're OK. We just can't wear our conscience on our sleeves!

And there's the constant colds. Why do we always get a cough around Christmas? Or what about the cycling accident that left the big scar on our leg? The cancer diagnosis we've now carried with us for years? Plus the side-effects of our medication for stress, which all but numbs us completely – and affects our sex life, too?

Or worse: The good friend who had an accident on holiday and didn't come back; our terminally ill parent we need to look after; the painful separation from our partner of 25 years. The trauma from childhood abuse.

And finally, the constant worries about money, which can make it so hard to breathe.

Love? Happiness?

Yes, it's still there, somewhere – beyond the trauma, the rejection, the loss, the suffering. But it's harder and harder to find. And certainly, it's not the dominant force.

There are good times, too. Success. Situations where we're winning. Maybe we're lucky enough not to have to worry about money, our job, our health, our family, or a partner.

But we rarely experience these things together. And even if we do, it can always change. How many times have we deeply enjoyed something, only to lose it again in an instant?

So, love is now paired with fear.

And more often than not, the latter is the dominant force. Our lives have become based on fear instead of love.

Haven't they?

When we look at the world outside, it's getting even worse: The demands people place on us, the stress levels, the resentment, the frustration, the misunderstandings, the lies – it's almost impossible to be ourselves.

Instead, we pretend and perform. It starts in our family, goes on to the workplace, our community, and further afield. We function, but ultimately end up feeling disconnected from ourselves.

Then we switch on the news and realise we're not the only ones who struggle. For a moment, this almost brings relief...until we feel worse again. We're bombarded by graphic images and detailed reports of violence and oppression, theft and murder, rape and torture, war and terror. We see the abuse of power on every level: corruption, selfishness. And famine, drought, floods, earthquakes. Starving children, devastated parents. During the week this paragraph was written, newspapers reported a man executed for demonstrating in favour of women's' rights, mass shootings, an explosion in a block of apartments, historical rape allegations. This is in addition to the daily coverage of economic downturn, climate crisis, the global pandemic, and huge streams of refugees in every part of the world.

The main headline, though, for several weeks, has been the elimination of team after team from the football world championships – showing devastated players, the resignation of the coach, and the despair of an entire country. We might even welcome this because we just can't cope with the other news anymore.

When it comes to the global perspective, it seems that even the notion of love has been completely eliminated.

The only way to cope with all this is to give in. We close down more and more, and try to carve out this little space around us where we can feel at least some love: romantically, through a hobby, in nature, holding a puppy, or watching a rom-com on TV.

At least much of what's happening is far away. We see it on the news, but (if we're lucky) we're in the safety of our living room, our car, our workplace, our tradition, our country.

We accept this as normal – and say things like, "that's life!". "It is what it is." "What can I do?" Why invest in something that can't be changed anyway?

Or we might even say, "it's just human nature".

So, we live in a world where love is reserved to a few rare, intimate moments – and belonging is defined by boundaries of culture, ethnicity, or nationality.

And yet, still we don't think we've lost the plot?

Are we HAPPY in the world we created? Personally, I don't know anyone who really is. We're resigned to the fact that "it is what it is". We may call it acceptance. Or inevitability.

But happy?

Let's recap – and state it as clearly as possible: We have accepted that life can never be entirely happy, neither on a personal level, nor as a society. Let alone on a global scale.

REALLY?

This is entirely unacceptable. It CAN be changed. And it must be changed.

B. THE WORLD AS IT COULD BE

We need to turn the entire experience upside down. We need…a REVOLUTION!

But (and this a is very large "but"), how do we want the world to be? What do we really want to create?

There was a reason behind the practical exercise at the beginning of the manifesto: to discover what we want for ourselves rather than to be told what it is. Otherwise, profound change would not be possible.

So, what did your heart tell you? What would a life that made you entirely happy look like? How would the world look?

I assume you visualised some images and ideas, and experienced a deep feeling of peace in your heart. But very likely it was just a glimpse, some obvious changes you'd make, rather than a very detailed picture. It's rather difficult to imagine a world free of the daily struggles and suffering we're used to.

Reading the description of our lives and world in the last chapter, it may even have dawned on you that the notion of overcoming this entirely is so radical, so entirely opposite to anything we've ever experienced, that it almost fills us with fear. Don't we *need* the opposites in our lives – good and bad, beautiful and ugly, demanding and easy – in order to judge and experience, to develop, to learn, to grow?

Wouldn't life be boring without it?

Well, change doesn't mean we need to give up what we enjoy. Why should we? In fact, we ought, rather, to focus on it. The only caveat is that our enjoyment mustn't come at the expense of others.

Many of our dreams are hard to believe possible (such as success, security, and prosperity) for everyone to attain because we're so used to thinking in terms of scarcity and limitation, rather than abundance. But even the science is clear on this matter: There is enough food, enough space to live in dignity, and enough work for everyone on this planet, not to mention the Cosmos.

We're not talking about giving up our individual identities, either. We can still have different tastes in art, food, music, whatever we enjoy. In fact, we must: Different life journeys and experiences are the main idea behind the creation of the universe! The archetypal forces, which will be explored later, play a significant role – when we tackle the tasks from the point of love rather than fear.

When we look at the media today, there's relentless criticism. We can switch from channel to channel, and the targets may differ, but criticism is the dominant – and often only – theme.

And it's become a habit in our lives, too. We find a journalist to voice the criticism on our behalf.

Voicing what we want instead is rather more difficult.

This new human experience is so contrary to everything we're used to that it's almost impossible to conjure up. But it *can* be experienced. And once we do, there will be no desire to turn the clock back.

To get a better idea, we should start with something we can easily agree on: What we *don't* want anymore; what we're happy to sacrifice. (And if there's still anyone out there who doesn't agree, they'll be convinced after the following experience.)

Let's imagine...

A world without wars, without torture, without violence, without rejection, without oppression.

A world without anger, without fear, without guilt, without shame.

A world without illnesses, without accidents, without disasters, without pain.

A world without hatred and division.

A world without suffering.

Instead...

A world where any differences are discussed in a decent, personal, respectful way, creating an outcome that's beneficial for everybody involved.

A world where we keep fun and diversity, creativity.

A world where we live in harmony with nature and other creatures; where we learn from nature, where we tap into its innate wisdom.

A world where we identify with our heart and our soul rather than our skin colour, religion, political opinions, or the cultures we were born into.

A world with freedom of thought and respect for differing opinions.

A world that's exploding with creativity and amazing experiences, not with disaster and trauma.

A world where happiness means sharing, so everyone can participate.

A world where everyone lives in peace, both within and around us.

So, just imagine that one day, maybe in 2043, twenty years after the publication of this manifesto, you wake up in the morning (and indeed every morning) without anxiety and pressure. You feel rested, energised, calm, positive, and excited about what the day is about to bring.

You can't wait to see your family and your neighbours, and look forward to the job you love. Your amazing abilities and creative input are truly valued.

You see the beauty and magnificence in difference and individuality.

You live in the knowledge that you are safe – and connected to the most powerful force in the universe: to love.

And you feel deeply happy.

If we let go of the scepticism – and agree on this goal – the only remaining question is how it can be achieved.

C. THE CASE FOR A REVOLUTION

As the world stands, we have three options:

1. *We carry on as before.* Try to muddle through. The problem is, things won't stay as they are. We've already entered a magnificent downward spiral: We're the first generation in world history with the potential to make life on this planet extinct; at least life as we know it. And we wouldn't only blow ourselves, humans and animals, up but the repercussions for us in spirit form would be enormous, too.

    Of course, we'd survive in spirit. But we'd have to restart, as we did when we first arrived on this planet, going through Stone Age, Iron Age, antiquity, medieval ages, Renaissance, Industrial Revolution, scientific breakthroughs, to where we are today: completely connected technologically, yet so divided in our minds that we threaten each other with nuclear bombs (another achievement of our amazingly advanced science). What's more, if nobody pushes the button, the slow-motion version has already started anyway, with environmental and climate change.

    In other words, this isn't a viable option.

2. *We opt out.* We become completely self-realised and enlightened, and return to the Source. In between, we pass through a state of non-attachment, of complete freedom, that in Buddhism is called Nirvana, until the entire universe is free of individual beings and can cease to exist.

    But there may be a problem: Are we really ready to give up life? Are we ready to never incarnate again? Are we ready to let go of individuality? Are we ready to let go of our soul family? Are we ready to stop playing?

    You may want to take a moment to re-read the above questions, replacing the "*we*" with "*I*", and ponder it in your heart.

    In the next chapter, it'll become clearer what an incredible construction we'd actually be leaving behind. But even though many religious and spiritual schools suggest we take this route, with very few exceptions, humankind doesn't seem to be ready for it.

    So, this isn't a viable option, either.

3. *We follow a third way.* If we're not ready to give up the human experience, but it's clear that we can't continue as we have before, there's only one way left: To make our human experience a more positive one.

    In other words, *change* is the only option. Radical, dramatic, immediate, change for the better.

Of course, there's hardly anyone who wouldn't agree that the world needs to change; that our lives could do with improvement, and humankind as a whole, as well.

This is how every revolution started. But how did they end? Normally in failure. Often, they replaced an oppressive system with an even worse one.

Usually, revolutions have sought to overturn the *circumstances*. And because *people* themselves didn't change, they always failed – or, in fact, rebounded on those who started it. Many revolutions succeeded though violence – which then violently backfired. They didn't bring more happiness; the roles of the oppressor and the oppressed were simply switched.

Take the French Revolution of 1789, inspired by the amazing period of enlightenment – with breakthroughs in philosophy, science, and democracy... From the first day of the Revolution – supposedly based on the values of liberty, equality, and brotherhood – the very same principles were violated. Since people were excluded from the Brotherhood, liberty remained limited, and the dominant factor was the desire for revenge.

Other revolutions failed before they even started because the headwind, the resistance from the establishment, was simply too strong.

The Reiki Revolution doesn't revolutionise the world. It revolutionises ourselves. Our understanding, our experiences.

It turns our self-awareness, our perception and, as a result, our behaviour, upside down. Not *re-acting* to the world, but *acting* from our hearts. And this means that every single step of the program, every single exercise, will lead to a noticeably happier, healthier, and more meaningful life.

The more people who join, the bigger the impact will be on our collective existence.

But if we really want to change the entire human experience – replacing fear with love as the dominant force – we need to reach a critical mass. Once we reach 15% of the population, we have a tipping point. And the whole of society can change.

(And, yes, as it currently stands, this is 1.2 billion people!)

We need help. And this is where Reiki comes in.

D. THE STORY BEHIND THE BOOK

The idea for the Reiki Revolution was born in 2020 during the first outbreak of COVID. A deeply frightening, yet at the same time somehow heart-opening experience: People phoned their distant relatives, checked on elderly neighbours, and grew closer together. There was suddenly huge recognition for those working in healthcare and other vital services, and for a moment it seemed as if society was shifting to more fairness and equality.

In the UK, this moment lasted about three months. Then the restrictions were eased, and everyone tried to get back to a degree of normality and leave the horrifying lockdown behind. In autumn, COVID hit back with a vengeance, another lockdown was introduced, and this time, the sense of community was completely forgotten.

When the questions were asked how COVID happened, an abundance of theories emerged, from bats to its accidental escape from an internationally financed research facility in China with poor safety standards.

But nobody asked *why* it really happened.

No matter how it physically started, on the level of collective consciousness, we, as humankind, created it. In fact, we *wanted* it. It was a cry for change – and could have become a huge turning point. A point at which we realise we can only solve problems when we stand together.

What happened, though, was the opposite: Families, communities, and indeed, nations, fell apart over COVID responses. Rather than trying to understand that everyone just wanted to do their best (at least, the majority), fingers were pointed, and arguments ensued.

In the end, the aggression turned on those desperately trying to find solutions to mitigate the outbreak and care for the sick.

Even spiritually minded people got caught up in physical theories, rather than looking at the deeper meaning: What can we *learn* from it?

As a result of the pandemic, global supply chains collapsed, poverty has increased, and the climate crisis is taking second place to desperate attempts to save our living standards. At the time of writing this, it's scarily obvious that, as so often is the case, that we haven't learned from it. The world hasn't changed for the better and is in many ways worse off post-COVID than it was before.

The pandemic also had a serious effect on the Reiki community.

For most Reiki practitioners, the cornerstone of their practice had been its use as a complementary therapy, for themselves, friends and family, and often also for clients. Some ran a professional practice, many others volunteered to give Reiki treatments in charities, hospitals, or hospices.

They were used to using Reiki as a tool to connect with other people. COVID put a stop to it. Complementary therapy clinics were forced to close, hospitals and hospices only let doctors and nurses continue to work there, and private practices were unable to stay open. Even though, remarkably, Reiki can be sent over a distance and physical contact – or even close proximity – isn't necessary, demand for treatments plummeted.

As a result, the impact on finances and mental health was felt in the Reiki community as much as anywhere else.

Personally, I was hit as well: It was impossible to continue offering in-person Reiki training, and the regulating bodies in the UK were categorical in their rejection of online training for professional purposes. In the end, I took this opportunity to finish my second book, detailing my personal journey with Reiki – and how I'd come to view this modality primarily as a door-opener to a spiritual awareness.

And suddenly things fell into place. This was what was needed: A program to bring this awareness into everyday life. To make Reiki a lifestyle.

It was a few days before Christmas, and I started to build a page on my website and send emails out. Two weeks later, 150 students had joined the "January Reiki Challenge", a program that included daily emails, with exercises, as well as weekly live coaching for the entire group.

I felt so strongly guided to offer this that I wasn't even deterred by the lack of planning. Often, the day before, I didn't know what the exercise for the next day would be, and sat at my computer until the early hours to complete the task. I followed my intuition, moving from topic to topic on issues we face on a daily basis – and the feedback was phenomenal. Following the comments in the Facebook group, the questions and stories revealed at the coaching, and the many emails I received, the month turned out to be life-changing. Of course, I was in the privileged position to join in with the exercises and witness the effects first-hand. Participants said it entirely changed their perspectives. It made them accept and love themselves again, cope with life, and find a different way of dealing with other people. It raised their happiness to a new level.

Some of the exercises I'd already tested in workshops over the years; others were completely new. The structure was based on scientific proof I discovered a few years ago about how Reiki worked on different vibrational levels.

Over the next two years, the program was refined, step by step, and eventually became structured along three steps to a happier and more meaningful life:

REALISATION – to realise experientially that we're eternal, multi-dimensional, and interconnected beings.

CHANGE – allowing this to change our perceptions and attitude towards ourselves and others.

APPLICATION – to bring this awareness into everyday life.

The key to it is the connection that Reiki creates: To higher vibrational levels in the universe. Indeed, all the way to the very Source.

And to experience that this connection is not something external, but written into our DNA.

The day I wrote this chapter (with increasing nervousness, given that the deadline was three weeks away), I received an email that couldn't have been more poignant:

Dear Torsten,

I am participating in the January Reiki Challenge, and I enjoy it very much.

I was introduced to Reiki 1 and 2 ten or eleven years ago, but I didn't do it regularly. I could not connect to the Source. I felt it was outside of my reach.

I even stopped giving self-treatments but last autumn something changed. I listened to your sessions on YouTube and decided to do Reiki on an everyday basis - give myself treatments.

Among other things, the connection became natural.

This lovely email wasn't just amazingly reassuring, it also confirmed one of my key experiences with Reiki: There are no coincidences.

(Including the fact that you are reading this book right now.)

E. HOW IT'S GOING TO WORK

Given that for millennia, the most amazing concepts, introduced to improve our lives, deepen our spiritual understanding, and change society (from the Vedic scriptures to religious teachings, shamanic practices, to the New Age movement, to simple decency), have had so little impact that the world remains in a constant state of suffering – why should this one now work?

For three reasons:

1. Reiki

We have help. The system of Reiki is a way to connect to universal guidance. In fact, in many exercises, we need do hardly any work ourselves. We just need to listen and experience. The next chapter gives an overview of Reiki, and why its real power has so strangely been overlooked for the past 100 years.

2. Understanding

To solve the problems, we need to understand how they developed in the first place, both in our lives and in the world. (And there is an astonishingly clear explanation in chapter 3.)

3. Experience

We can't give love if we never received it. We need to *experience*. Therefore, in this program, every step is experiential; nothing needs to be believed. This is what the majority of this book, Parts 2 and 3, is dedicated to.

No outer pressure can be applied. Even if people don't change, they won't end up in hell. Because there isn't one. The only hell we can experience is the fear, separation, and lack of love we go through in our earthly experience. Again and again, incarnation after incarnation.

But the inner pressure is there: We *want* a happier and more meaningful life. And we don't want to see others suffering, either. (And if there are exceptions, they will change over time, once they experience that they're loved, too.)

This program can make the change. ALL the change. It can create a life and a society built on happiness rather than survival.

We're the first generation in human history that can make these changes:

> A. Everyone can access information about world history (including wars, slavery, rape, oppression, and destruction); we have the knowledge of our family histories and the struggles they experienced; and we can access our own past lives through regression techniques. In other words, we know where our individual and collective trauma is rooted.

> B. Science and spirituality are so advanced that we can understand the bigger picture: The idea behind the creation of the universe.

C. We have the technical means to reach people simultaneously, all over the globe, to reach the critical mass needed.

D. We have techniques like Reiki that give us a tangible, spiritual connection. And they are accessible to all, not just a secretive few.

E. We have enough experience with democracy to allow for participation of everyone in society.

My intuition was very clear about two things: Firstly, we have only 20 years to turn things around. And secondly, we *will* succeed.

For the program in this book to work, four "instructions" are essential:

A. Read slowly

The information in this book alone can already change our perception. But it needs time to register. Please stop regularly, and let it sink in. If a sentence feels important to you, read it twice.

B. Do the exercises

Please don't carry on reading without finishing the exercise in the previous chapter. They build on each other.

C. Repeat

Each time you do an exercise, it'll go deeper. Our subconscious is made up of layers, and some trauma or deeply rooted beliefs can take repeated attempts to reach them. If, initially, you work through this book in a week, I recommend taking a month next time, doing one exercise a day.

D. Be completely honest

Ultimately, all the answers can be found inside of you. Therefore, there is *nothing* you need to hold back. Even though it can be helpful to go on this journey together – with a friend, a partner, your children, or even a colleague – please respect each other's privacy. There will be several realisations that are rather personal, and you may not want to share them.

Many of the exercises can be done even if you haven't learned Reiki. Simply replace the word "Reiki" with "universe". Regardless, the deepest change will be achieved when Reiki is involved.

2.

Why Reiki can help

A. PERSONAL STORY

The system of Reiki is just over 100 years old, and for the majority of that time, has been significantly misunderstood.

It's renowned all over the world as a complementary therapy, even though the improvement of physical conditions is only a side effect. Once we uncover what it's really designed to do, it opens a whole new world – and, indeed, can explain the world *and* our individual places in it.

As soon as people begin learning Reiki, though, they embark on a personal journey. So, in order to explain its real depth, I feel I need to share, briefly, my own story; especially as I'm probably a rather unlikely proponent of Reiki.

After all, I don't like herbal teas; after several failed attempts, I gave up on meditation in my teens; and until my mid-30s, I had no idea what the word "spirituality" really stood for. I'd always considered myself "mainstream" rather than "alternative".

From a very early age, though, I had a strong interest in religion – primarily because I hoped my questions about life (its meaning and why it was so unjust) would be answered. Born in north Germany, the dominant religion was Lutheran Christianity and I was deeply fascinated by Martin Luther's life story and achievements. After school, I even studied theology for one-and-a-half years, but then realised that being a reverend wasn't the right job for me. After a stint in the German army (which was compulsory at the time), I discovered my fascination with politics, became chairman of a party in my local constituency, and ended up obtaining a degree in political sciences at Hamburg University.

Though my main interest lay in practical politics, I enjoyed the academic and scientific approaches (which is probably where my tendency to put things in bullet-point lists derives – as is obvious throughout this book!). I was fascinated by the idea of democracy and how it would be possible to engage a large number of people to actively participate in the organisation of society.

But somehow my entrepreneurial streak came through also, which I combined with my love of art and antiques, and, parallel to attending university, I started a business. After a few years, I was organising retail shows for English antiques and silver in every major German city.

Following my degree, I turned another dream into reality and moved to London. I'd visited so many times already on my buying trips, and, suddenly, I lived in this amazing city – as the proud owner of an apartment in trendy in Notting Hill and, eventually, a retail store on London's famous Regent Street. I added my own jewellery designs to the portfolio and, having just turned 30, felt on top of the world.

Then everything went downhill: Foot-and-Mouth disease, an epidemic not unlike COVID, but affecting cows and sheep rather than humans, took a grip of Britain. As a result, tens of thousands of animals were slaughtered and the pictures of them being burned in huge piles were disseminated around the world. I seem to have been the only one with no real idea of the extent of the problem, because I didn't (and still don't) watch television. But everybody else had, including American tourists, who stayed away from London. Which is when I realised that they had made up 80% of my customer base. Suddenly, it was down to 20%. And with my enormous overheads, this was unsustainable.

I tried anything and everything to come up with creative, new business ideas, and even won a contract to design jewellery for a French fashion house. But it was too little, too late. The business went into bankruptcy – and I followed. I lost the apartment in Notting Hill, my apartment in Berlin, and even the family home in Hamburg, as my parents had guaranteed the loans.

The worst of it was that Mum had joined me in London a year after I moved there, and lived just around the corner from me, in Notting Hill. We'd run the business together and both loved designing jewellery. Now we had one more thing in common: No home. Had it not been for friends offering us their guest bedrooms, we would have ended up homeless.

A few months later, we seemed to have reached a turning point, and found a small house to rent. We were ready to restart our lives and get back into business.

Except, it didn't happen. Having sold our collection of antiques, and the remains of the jewellery business (including Mum's wedding band), we were back to square one. Neither my attempts to start a new business nor my hunt for a new job worked out. Eventually, I worked in a supermarket during the day and as a cleaner in the evening but still could not make ends meet. We were falling into arrears with the rent and on the brink of eviction again.

I pondered over my life: Youngest head prefect in my school's history; youngest local chairman of my political party; a respected university degree; the best earner amongst the wider family for many years; a store in one of London's most famous locations. And now, hardly able to provide for the most basic needs. There were days when we had barely enough food.

I'd tried anything I could think of to change the situation. Nothing had worked.

Suicide seemed the only way out.

Mum and I were sitting in our cramped living room, and I was so tired I couldn't even cry. I just said, "I can't go on anymore. I want to get out. What... if we just ended our lives?"

Mum and I had always been super-close. We had similar tastes, hobbies, and interests. But this time, but she disagreed. "I completely understand. I feel exactly the same... but we can't do this. It isn't just about us. We will affect other people as well..."

I also had second thoughts. Unlike Mum, it wasn't to do with other people, but very much to do with myself. A while ago, I'd read a book called Conversations with God, by Neale Donald Walsch. It had a huge impact on my thinking and introduced me to the idea that this life may, indeed, be just one of many.

So, if I shortened the experience in this one, I might have to go through a similar problem again in the next one, to learn my lesson. As hilarious as it sounds, this was the last thing I wanted. Then, somehow, I had to muddle through. I began to work seven days a week, and we got another chance from the landlords to repay the rental arrears over a longer period.

During this time, my sister was a student in Germany and while still studying, tried to help as much as she could. Finances, of course, were very limited but she tried to help as much as possible in other ways, always lending an ear and trying to encourage us with inspirational books. One of them, which she sent to Mum, was the autobiography of a German policeman who happened to practice Reiki.

Mum was fascinated. Reiki could bring change? Normal people could learn it? You automatically got "healing hands"? She *had* to learn it herself, and somehow managed to put a few coins aside every week until she had saved the fee for a course.

It was around that time when I overheard some people at the estate agents I did the cleaning for: They were looking for someone to refurbish one of the apartments they managed. This would pay better than cleaning! I obviously volunteered convincingly – and got the job. It took three times longer than I'd anticipated but everybody was happy with the result. Soon, I was offered more jobs like this. And slowly our life got back on track: We moved to a slightly bigger home, the ageing car got repaired, and the rental arrears were settled.

About a year later, I took a moment to look back at this period – and only then did the astonishing realisation occur: I remembered how apologetic Mum had been when I landed my first refurbishment job. It had started on a Friday, and she wasn't around to give me any support.

It was the day that her Reiki course started. The VERY DAY Reiki came into our lives, our lives changed for the better. Profoundly.

Of course, one might categorise this as a beautiful coincidence – but having trained over 10,000 students now myself, I can say that dramatic, tangible, and life-enhancing change is not the exception. It's the norm. The hallmark of Reiki.

In a large-scale survey of over 1,000 Reiki practitioners, by the ReikiScience Academy in 2022, 95% answered that Reiki turned their lives in a more positive direction.

When Mum came back from her Reiki course, she did some rather weird things. She placed her hands on anything and everything: Our dog, the house plants, and on me. For a back problem, headaches, a bruise on my arm, or just when I was stressed or tired.

I could immediately feel an unusual warmth – and very tangible results. Of course, Mum urged me to learn Reiki as well. But why should I learn a *complementary therapy*? I had to make money and get our lives back on track.

Well, if Mum is convinced that something's good for you, she'll find a way to make it happen. So, I got my first Reiki course for Christmas that year.

B. WHAT IS REIKI?

Reiki is one of the world's best-known energy healing systems. Originating in Japan, it's astonishing for several reasons, even to those who use it regularly because:

1. It's so simple
Reiki can be learned by anybody. And within minutes.

All that's needed is an attunement – a short energetic opening given by a Reiki Master – and the flow of Reiki (high vibrational energy) begins. The practitioner acts as a channel for this energy.

Traditionally, it's taught in three levels, to allow enough time to gain experience and confidence, and to become accustomed to the higher vibrational levels. But even after the initial attunement, Reiki can be used straight away.

Reiki is then activated by intention: As soon as the practitioner states, "I intend to connect to Reiki", the connection is there and most people feel an immediate energetic sensation in their palms, often as tingling or warmth.

Reiki can be used on oneself or other people, animals, or objects, by a simple laying on of the hands. No physical manipulation is involved; the hands can also be kept slightly away from the body, or Reiki can be sent over a distance. The client stays fully clothed.

As soon as the hands are placed, Reiki starts working, and the practitioner becomes a mere facilitator or, indeed, an *observer* of the treatment. While sometimes results can be achieved in minutes, the usual time for a treatment is between twenty minutes and an hour. For severe or chronic illnesses, or deep-rooted problems, several treatments are usually recommended.

Reiki can also be given using the breath, the eyes, or the practitioner's energy field.

2. It supports physical healing

Reiki is known to promote physical healing: Several peer-reviewed papers, in addition to surveys and well-documented case studies, have confirmed that it can be beneficial for any physical condition. It's not necessarily an alternative therapy but is often used as a complementary treatment alongside conventional methods.

It can significantly reduce pain, improve healing times (especially after surgery), and reduce the side-effects of medication and chemotherapy.

Reiki is assumed to stimulate the body's self-healing responses, and has been accepted officially within the British NHS (National Health Service). It's offered in over 800 hospitals in the United States, and the accident department of Berlin's University Hospital now has a number of fully employed Reiki practitioners. The hospital had run a study where a number of complementary therapies were introduced to patients. As the approval rate for Reiki was by far the highest, they decided to offer this beneficial treatment long-term.

In the above-mentioned survey of over 1,000 Reiki practitioners, more than 91% responded that Reiki improved their physical health.

Detailed medical knowledge is not necessary to give a Reiki treatment, as it's non-intrusive and the energy will automatically go where it's needed. There are no side-effects or contraindications when used on its own.

3. It works holistically

Even though it's beneficial for physical ailments, to a huge degree the appeal of Reiki lies in the fact that it works holistically. Beyond the reach of conventional therapies. It doesn't just address a symptom, it addresses the root cause of the problem.

As the physical body is an integrated system, the practitioner may be drawn to other areas than the ones where a symptom is felt, e.g., a back problem may be rooted in a knee issue; a knee problem may be the result of the hips being out of alignment.

And of course, someone's lifestyle has a huge influence on their physical health, whether it's stress or traumatic experiences, unhealthy habits or anger, sadness or circumstantial problems.

Recipients of Reiki often feedback that they've become aware of these connections, and the symptoms are eased as a result.

4. It reduces stress

Clients often fall asleep during a treatment – or report that it's helped them to find a healthy sleeping pattern again.

Reiki helps people to relax and let go of stress, anxiety, and sadness. It measurably lowers the stress hormones in the body and allows recipients to cope better with the demands of everyday life.

It often leads to a change in one's perception, uncovering a deeper meaning in our experiences and allowing us to learn from them and move on.

It may also help to accept situations that can't currently be changed, by revealing a new way of dealing with them.

Again, in the survey, 92% of respondents answered that Reiki improved their stress levels, whilst 95% said Reiki improved their mental wellbeing.

5. It increases intuition

During a Reiki treatment, clients often have new insights and ideas; it increases intuition and inner guidance, and can lead to more clarity in their lives. (Many exercises in this book are based on this potential.)

People often gain more clarity about their personal journeys, enabling them to make positive changes.

6. It's a spiritual door-opener

While focussing on the "healing hands" in a treatment and observing what Reiki is doing, it acts as a complementary therapy. However, when we try to trace the energy back to its origin, we realise that a connection has been opened to higher vibrational levels in the universe. Thus, Reiki becomes a path to a deeper spiritual understanding, and self-discovery.

Again, the survey showed astonishing results: 93% of people said Reiki had enhanced their spiritual understanding, while 94% felt more connected to the universe.

Reiki helps us not just to realise we are spiritual beings, but to *experience* ourselves as such, as souls in a body.

7. It works beyond time and space

Reiki helps to go beyond the boundaries of the three-dimensional experience in a very practical way: A treatment can be "sent" over any distance, and even forwards and backwards through time.

It works at the quantum level.

8. It's not a belief system

Reiki is "learning by doing". It's not a belief system, nor is it necessary to accept certain explanations in order to benefit from it.

It works with any religion, as well as for those who do not follow one.

Because of all these benefits, a staggering 99% of participants in the ReikiScience Academy survey said they would recommend learning Reiki to others.

A more detailed introduction to Reiki can be found in my first book, *Reiki Made Easy*.

C. REIKI HISTORY

The system of Reiki was born in 1922 when Japanese monk Mikao Usui had a deeply transformational experience after three weeks of fasting and meditating on a mountain.

Up to that point, his life had been a bit of a roller coaster: After a highly successful career as a businessman, when he turned 50, his fortunes shifted and he became bankrupt. Married with two children, he was unable to get back on track and support his family. Traditional Japanese values meant he lost any social standing and became an outcast in society.

After several failed attempts to rebuild his business, he eventually accepted there might be a deeper reason for its failure. It could be an opportunity to take his life in a different direction. So, he joined a succession of monasteries in Kyoto, with the idea of not just understanding what life is all about intellectually, but experientially discovering its meaning. He was hoping to reach the state of Anshin Ritsumei – of complete inner independence and peace. But the various practices in the monasteries failed to help him get there.

Eventually, he withdrew to Mount Kurama, a famous spiritual place near Kyoto, with the intention to completely surrender. He risked being frozen to death or being attacked by wild animals, which the region is known for.

After twenty-one days of enduring the wilderness, he suddenly felt himself surrounded by light – so bright that he described it as blinding – and had to lie down and close his eyes. He felt a deep connection to the universe, which he later described as Rei-Ki – and experienced forgiveness, acceptance and love. You might say that he felt *one* with the universe.

In Japanese, this is called *Satori*: a moment of enlightenment or of sudden understanding. He experienced what it means to be a spiritual being incarnated in a body, being fully aware of both levels of existence.

On his descent back into civilisation, he caught his toe on an exposed root and tore off a toenail, resulting in a painful wound. In the absence of any medical aid, he placed his hands around the wound using *teate* – traditional Japanese palm healing. However, the result was much stronger than he'd expected, and he realised that his experience had not only allowed him a spiritual connection but also access to remarkable healing powers.

Having tried this out on friends and family, within a few weeks he moved his family to Tokyo and opened a small practice to give Reiki treatments. And he began to develop a way of passing this gift on to students, so they could offer treatments as well. The result is the system that today we call "Reiki".

Usui himself only described it as "based on Reiki", which at the time was a word used to describe the highest level of existence in the universe. *Rei* can best be translated as *"spiritual"*, *Ki* as *"life force energy"*.

The turning point of his system came with an earthquake in 1923. The Kanto earthquake, named after the plain Tokyo was built on, became the biggest natural disaster in Japanese history, claiming 170,000 lives. As hundreds of thousands were wounded, for several weeks Mikao Usui went on daily walks around the city and offered Reiki to many of them. The astonishing results led to a public breakthrough of his system, and it became more and more popular. Over the following years, he fine-tuned his teachings and added symbols as access codes to the different vibrational levels on which Reiki works, because he realised that it worked not just on the physical, but also on mental and emotional issues, and brought a deeper connection between practitioners and clients, as well as enabling them to feel a connection to higher energetic levels in the universe.

By the time of his death in 1926, Mikao Usui had trained over 2,000 students; among them, 21 to the master level. These masters were then able to give attunements and pass on this healing ability to other students, creating the most important feature for the authenticity and integrity of the system today: A lineage. Every student of the Usui System of Reiki is given a lineage and can trace this back to the founder.

D. REIKI SYMBOLS

Mikao Usui soon realised that the gift he received was much more complex and multi-layered than merely a more intense version of the palm-healing tradition of *teate*. Otherwise, he would not have insisted that the level of energy involved was the highest in the universe – where creator and creation meet – and termed it "Reiki".

Over time (quite soon after his death), this awareness became rather diluted, and more focus was placed on using Reiki as a complementary therapy, albeit working in a holistic spectrum. One could argue that this was the exact reason why this system, unlike so many others, not only survived but gained enormous traction.

But in this process, the important role of the Reiki *symbols* has been entirely overlooked.

And of course, many people (including myself) feel rather uneasy when it comes to the idea of symbols. They tend to be associated with secret organisations or cults – even though we use symbols every day in our lives. The dollar sign or the drawing of a heart are symbols because, unlike a word, they do not have a meaning in themselves. They stand for something *else*. And much as the image of a heart can invoke feelings of love, so can the Reiki symbols make us aware of what we have hidden inside of us.

They stand for the different levels of the human experience (or, indeed, existence), and are incredibly powerful tools. Or, rather, *keys*. They're designed to help us understand and direct the level at which Reiki works.

Traditionally, they're introduced at Level 2 in Reiki training – once the student has gained enough experience to sense the vibrational subtleties of the system. The concept is that there are three levels of human experience: the physical, the spiritual, and the collective.

The Power Symbol

(A later-assumed, Western name of the symbol.) This stands for the physical existence, the *level of form*. Once it's drawn, the mantra repeated, or it's invoked by sound, the focus of the Reiki treatment is on physical healing and material change.

The Harmony Symbol

(Again, a Western name.) It stands for the non-physical levels of existence: The emotional, mental, and spiritual. It helps to deal with emotions, shifts the point of perception, and allows access to intuition and guidance. It ultimately stands for the awareness that there is more to a human existence than just the physical.

The Connection Symbol

(Often also referred to as the distance symbol.) This is probably the most misunderstood of the symbols. Commonly used to enable distant treatments, its real function is to bring the awareness that space (and time) is a temporary experience, and that it's in everybody's power to transcend this and connect to the level where the entire human experience is connected. One could call it applied quantum physics.

In my Reiki 2 courses, I always pair the students up for a distant treatment then leave the recipients in one room, and gather the rest of the practitioners in another, from where they send a distant Reiki treatment to their respective partner. The incredulity and excitement when they give each other feedback is simply extraordinary – and for many it's the moment when the last doubts about Reiki disappear.

Not only do the practitioners feel a connection – and the receivers feel the physical experiences and healing effects in their body – but practitioners often receive an intuitive insight about the client's physical problems and emotional state.

E. REIKISCIENCE

In 2016, I undertook a research project at the Hagalis Institute in Switzerland, to gain an understanding as to whether Reiki worked independently of any potential placebo effects.

Most scientific studies focus on humans (with the interesting exception of a project involving rats, which showed that Reiki treatments significantly reduce stress hormones), and therefore might be open to the suggestion that the very fact that therapists spend time with the client could in itself influence the perception and, therefore, the result. This is why in some newer studies, a proportion of participants receive "sham Reiki". However, most studies cover "soft" results, such as anxiety and quality of sleep, rather than blood samples or indicators of physical healing.

For many years, I asked my Reiki students to do a "water test": To fill two glasses with tap water, place their hands around one of them and give it Reiki for a few minutes, and then taste the difference between the two. Many students have used this with friends and family. The overwhelming feedback is that the water tastes softer, smoother, and more pleasant.

The Hagalis Institute analyses the quality of water – particularly bottled mineral water and the effect of water filtering systems – using a novel technology. After undergoing a process of filtering and condensation, drops of water are placed on a glass dish and allowed to dry. The residual minerals and trace elements are subsequently analysed under a microscope.

What resulted exceeded all expectation: The experiments not only confirmed the efficacy of Reiki but, in fact, opened a new chapter into the history of its use.

The first experiment used "simple Reiki": Two bottles were filled with local tap water, one as a neutral sample, the other to be treated with Reiki. The Reiki treatment was timed at 60 minutes, and chosen to simulate a Reiki treatment as it's usually applied in clinical settings.

The analysis determined the sample water as mid-quality tap water, safe for human consumption. On a scale from 1 (the best) to 6 (undrinkable and heavily polluted), it measured 3.1.

After an hour of Reiki, the quality of the water had improved to 1.9 – normally the entry level of natural spring water!

Encouraged by this result, a few weeks later we took the experiments to another level: I gave the water a number of further treatments, each time focusing on a Reiki symbol, to see whether this would make any difference.

The results were mind-blowing.

After focussing for 60 minutes on the Power Symbol, crystallisation was clearly observable throughout the entire water sample. Reiki had influenced the entire physical composition of the water.

Using the Harmony Symbol, pronounced crystallisation was found mainly at the edges of the water sample – as if it were pointing to something beyond physical existence.

Analysing the two tests, even the director of the institute concluded that the "Power experiment" seems to have employed a modality related to physical improvement, whilst the "Harmony experiment" was obviously working on a different level. It was abundantly clear: The tests had shown that Reiki worked on different vibrational levels.

However, the results using the Connection Symbol were the most fascinating: The crystals that formed were not only the largest and most refined, but also even touched and overlapped – giving almost a visual idea of the word "connection". In this experiment, the water quality improved even further, to 1.8.

Prior to the experiments, I'd already researched the Eastern understanding of T*anden* points (*Dantien* in Chinese), the main energy centres at the heart of practices like Chi Gong and Tai Chi. It was now clear that Reiki worked on the same understanding: The physical human body is connected to different vibrational levels through these non-physical centres – and the symbols offer a way to activate them. The lower Tanden is located just below the navel, the upper Tanden between the eyebrows, and the central Tanden at the level of the heart.

Based on this discovery, I created a new training program called ReikiScience, with the name not only referring to the fact that Reiki can be scientifically proven, but, and more importantly, that Reiki was a science in itself. It's able to identify different vibrational levels in the universe: the level of form for our physical, earthly existence, the spiritual level, and the connection between all things The training included several exercises, some of which are found in this book, to align with these vibrational levels by opening the respective Tanden centres.

The training became a full weekend course (as well as a video-based online training programme) and also included an attunement which focussed on the Tanden points.

Once again, the feedback was totally unexpected: Participants noticed a difference from other Reiki attunements they'd received, including those performed at the master level. They experienced a deep sense of peace and connection, were overwhelmed by emotions of love, and often saw themselves surrounded by the colour magenta.

Many commented that it had taken their Reiki to a new level and allowed them to feel a deeper connection as a result.

It has since become clear that the ReikiScience attunements can raise the vibrational level of the heart chakra beyond the previously connected frequency.

The entire program of the Reiki Revolution is based on this discovery. Ultimately, it's a revolution of the heart – enabling us not to live *with* but *from* our heart. It re-aligns our heart with the universe.

Images of the Reiki and water experiments can be found at: www.thereikirevolution.com.

F. REIKI AND RELIGIONS

About 60% of the world's population would describe themselves as religious, and I feel it's safe to assume that a significant further proportion is influenced by the religious tradition they were born into. So, we may be looking at 80 - 90% of people on this planet for whom religion plays an important role in their worldview, and it's therefore essential to understand the relationship between Reiki (or, indeed, the philosophical ideas in this book) and world religions.

It's also vital to state that Reiki can work with any religious belief – and isn't a new religion, or a sect, in itself. Mikao Usui travelled extensively, within Asia as well as to Europe and the USA, and was well aware of cultural differences. This allowed him to make sure that his healing system could be used in any culture, no matter what its religious background was.

In fact, Reiki can help us understand the spiritual essence of our chosen religion and aid the ultimate realisation that all religions have the same goal at their core: The understanding of an existence beyond the three-dimensional world, and to find a path to connecting with this "higher power".

As, by definition, there can only be one source of the universe, the differences between the religious teachings tend to be more semantic in nature: It's about different names, not different concepts.

G. THE REIKI PRINCIPLES

Reiki is primarily about experience, and its teaching includes techniques rather than dogma. But Mikao Usui, its founder, made one exception: He asked his students to repeat a set of five principles every morning and evening, as this would help them bring the awareness of higher vibrational energy into everyday life. On the memorial stone erected in his honour in 1927, they're written as follows:

Just for today

do not be angry,

do not worry,

be grateful,

work with diligence,

be kind to others.

Often mistaken as diktats, they actually show the journey through the vibrational levels. Of course, they also provide a moral compass, but they're mainly supposed to remind Reiki students to be more aware of how their daily conduct affects their energy.

Anger and *worry* are purely connected to the physical life, and therefore hold us in this range of experience. They can keep us stuck in the past, unable to create a more positive future.

Gratitude can kickstart a vibrational shift, and immediately creates a more positive attitude.

Diligence comes when we realise that we are, at our core, spiritual beings – and act accordingly.

And *kindness* is another way of acting from our heart: The highest vibration in the universe.

These principles are ways to raise our vibration towards more happiness and connection. And unlike, as is often the case with rules and regulations, they don't come with any punishment attached. They're nothing but helpful suggestions.   The introduction, *"just for today"*, makes this clear: It recognises that, as human beings, we not only have free will, but we often do things we regret. The Reiki principles leave no space for regrets. We simply try again.

Just for today, try to implement them. Make them the foundation upon which you go through your day. If, at the end of it, you realise that there have been a number of lapses, be assured, there'll be another day, another opportunity. Don't beat yourself, don't put yourself down, don't allow the thought that you're not good enough to enter your mind.

Instead, accept that you've tried. And if you try even more, the vibrational rise and happiness becomes increasingly powerful. This is the theme of the entire Reiki Revolution Manifesto. The more we work on it, the more it becomes reality.

H. LEARNING REIKI

As long as a student is part of a lineage extending back to Mikao Usui, the Japanese founder of the system of Reiki, it doesn't really matter how they've learned it.

I spent well over a decade trying to unearth the "original Reiki", but eventually reached the point where I realised there's currently no such thing as an absolute original Reiki – at least not in a way that's been shared with the rest of the world.

However, over the past 20 years, in addition to several reasonably authentic traditions, a number of offshoots have emerged. In most cases, different ideas and techniques were added but the core remained unchanged. Additionally, a few new healing techniques have also been created that have been called "Reiki" without having any connection to the original system. As the name *Reiki* can't be trademarked, ultimately anyone can create an energy or healing system and call it "Reiki".

As valuable as these may be, only Reiki with an original Usui lineage is valid for insurance purposes, acceptance in mainstream healthcare and scientific studies. Therefore, any information in this book is solidly based on the use of Reiki traditions going back to Mikao Usui.

The most important aspect of Reiki teaching is the attunement: the initial connection to Reiki. And this can be done in minutes.

What's essential though, is to gain confidence and experience. This is why a Reiki course is normally run over a weekend, to learn more about the history, background, idea of holistic healing, and particularly to start practising, get feedback and discuss the experiences with an experienced Reiki teacher.

Traditionally, Reiki has been structured along three levels:

Reiki 1, *Shoden* in Japanese, is the beginner's level. The connection is created, some background information about its history, holistic healing and energy are given, and practical exercises placing the hands in different positions complete the training.

Level 2, *Okuden* in Japanese (the inner teachings), is normally offered a few weeks or even months after Reiki 1. Although this isn't set in stone, it's advisable to have some experience using Reiki at the first level, as Level 2 marks a huge step in higher vibrational energy. It fine-tunes the practice, reveals how it works on different levels, and introduces the three Reiki symbols. In my courses, I add a number of exercises to sense the different vibrational levels at which Reiki works and to deepen my students' intuition – as well as offering information about how to practice professionally.

The third level, Reiki Master (*Shinpiden* – the "mystery teachings" – in Japanese) is sometimes split into two: A Master Practitioner and Master Teacher level, although traditionally, as I usually do it, this is taught in one course. It covers every aspect of Reiki history, philosophy and practice from a teacher's perspective, and includes step-by-step training on how to give an attunement to other people. Most Reiki Master students don't train in order to teach, but with the desire to understand the system of Reiki in all its complexity. Over time, though, many at least attune their children, partner, or friends.

To use the Reiki Revolution program, only the very first level is necessary. If we really want to change the world in a timely manner, and reach 1.2 billion people, access needs to be as simple and affordable as possible. Although I'd wholeheartedly recommend training to the first two traditional levels.

For me, therefore, it felt right to break with tradition and create a very short (three-hour) online Reiki introduction course that includes a distant attunement, so anybody can use it for themselves straight away.

For professional practice, though, traditional training is still necessary. There are many wonderful Reiki teachers all over the world; please follow your intuition to find the right one for you. I also offer live and online training myself – including the new, ReikiScience course.

3.

Why is the world as it is?

A. THE SET-UP OF THE UNIVERSE

After my years of research into Reiki – and the creation of the Reiki Challenge program – I felt it was time to share it more widely.

As soon as restrictions were partially lifted following COVID, I took the first opportunity I could to get to the United States, and booked myself into an Airbnb in Los Angeles for three months. Enough time, I thought, to lay the ground.

But it turned out that my own ground wasn't ready. It didn't work at all – and the global frustration after COVID took hold of me as well. I didn't make any meaningful contacts, the course venue I'd rented and already prepaid before COVID had gone bankrupt, friends I'd hoped who could help had moved away or passed away. Wherever I went to seek out opportunities or make connections turned out to be a dead end. Many venues were still closed due to the pandemic. The fact that I was just draining money added to the worries...the fear of bankruptcy was still deeply ingrained in my subconscious.

Los Angeles itself had changed, too. When I'd visited a few years before, I'd been amazed by the openness of the people, the welcoming atmosphere, the positive buzz. Now, there was division, no matter where I went or with whom I spoke – from people in a supermarket to Uber drivers or friends.

Rather than identifying as Californians – which I'd been used to – people now identified with whatever placed a division between themselves and others. Lines were established along political views, religions, traditions, skin colours, income, education, accents, and even regional borders. They had no interest, even, in listening to the other side. The stronger their own opinion, the better.

Many people were still involved in charitable projects – but even those (at least the ones I found) showed little interest beyond themselves; especially not in international issues. "Life on the ground" was demanding enough.

Rather than bringing us together again, COVID had done the opposite. But, of course, this realisation didn't help much with my project. As I had to be back in London, I could only stay for three months in the end; and the closer I got to my departure, the more frustrated I became.

I ended up spending most of my time working on the Reiki Challenge programme, which became clearer and clearer in its structure. Eventually, I offered the first mid-year challenge to my online students. The feedback was even more intense than before, and the idea emerged of turning it into a book. It would work so well on a bigger scale – like ground rules for living in LA. Or the world.

By the time the challenge was over, I only had a few weeks left in LA. Why did I not get anywhere over here?

In the end, I gave up. Literally. I sat down on the sofa in my little apartment, placed my hands together, and addressed the universe: "I don't understand why my plans didn't work. I don't know what I did wrong. But I accept that it wasn't meant to be. There's nothing left I can think of. I surrender. Completely. Entirely.

"Please take over."

I'd expected to sit for a while and hopefully feel better by surrendering to not being in charge anymore. Instead, I was bathed in blue light. When I opened my eyes again, it was still there. Over the next few days, it was a constant companion.

At some stage, I asked whether this was a guide. It said no. It was an Archangel. Michael.

There was no other interaction…I just waited, stunned by the enormous power I felt. When I looked up, the light-being appeared as high as the Eiffel tower (and of strangely similar shape).

But still nothing happened. I'd accepted that, if anything were to happen, I wasn't meant to be the one to instigate it. Then, a few days later, the blue light disappeared.

Instead, there was white light. Bright, clear light. Not a being, just light.

And there was a voice (or intuition?) saying, "If you want to change the world, you need to understand why it's like this in the first place." And little by little, I was told the set-up of the universe.

How right! We can only change the *how* if we know the *why*.

It's probably the biggest question of all times: Why can life be such a nightmare? Why is there so much suffering, heartbreak, illness? Natural disasters? Accidents? Unfulfillment? Depression? Overwhelm? Unhappiness? And indeed, so little love in the world...

In philosophy, as well as Christian theology, this is called the *Theodicy* question: Where's the righteousness in God's actions? Is there any? Why do some suffer while others seem to have everything? Why is there so much evil in this world?

The answer is as clear as it is shocking (and it's not the one Leibniz came up with): The world isn't just the way it is because we created it so – through focussing on ourselves rather than the common good, or due to oversight, negligence, misunderstanding, or fear – but because we actually *wanted* it this way.

Let me sum this up in a declaration:

**If we want to change the world,
we need to change what we want.
We need to *consciously un-want* the experience we're
having.**

To understand *what* we want (or wanted), though, we need to go all the way back to the beginning of time.

We need to understand the creation and set-up of the universe.

During my experience in Los Angeles, the universe was explained to me as *seven levels of existence*. For the purpose of this book, I include the basics of this concept, as it will help to understand the aims of the Reiki Revolution.

Even if it doesn't make sense in its entirety at present, please read on. The concept will be brought alive through the exercises to come...

The Seventh Level

The beginning of the universe wasn't a bang. It was nothing physical at all. The universe started as an *idea*. And an idea requires someone who has it in their mind.

This is the first level of the existence of the universe. But it's not *some*one. It's *every*one.

Because the seventh level is ALL that is. Therefore, nothing can be outside of it. It simply is *everything* – and it's eternal.

Philosophically, one could say it simply *IS*. It hasn't been created, but is the source of all creation.

This level isn't really a level because it *includes* everything. It's impossible to detach from it. (And therefore, no one can ever be "lost". Only blind.)

What we call this often depends on our viewpoint or tradition. A religious person may use the names of *Allah*, *God*, *Yahweh*, *Brahma*, the *Supreme Being*, or *The Divine*. Contemporary spiritualists might use the words of *The Source*, *Higher Power*, *Universe*, or *All-That-Is*. In science, the word that makes most sense would be *"singularity"* – used by one of the world's most respected academics, the mathematician and cosmologist, Stephen Hawking. He devoted much of his life to researching black holes – and his original assumption was that energy gets lost in them.

Eventually, he came to a radically different conclusion (which I'm paraphrasing here). He accepted that everything is born out of a singularity, and then develops into different vibrational levels: An unlimited number of different energetic strands; constant expansion and development.

At some stage, this development – *our creation* – moves in the other direction and condenses again. In a black hole, with enormous force, all this is then compressed into a singularity. Infinite density.

All individuality ceases to exist.

But what stays, Hawking suggested, is the *memory*, the knowledge.

The Sixth Level

This takes us to the sixth level, the *level of creation*. It can best be described as the *idea*. The structure. The cosmic laws.

To understand this level means to understand the universe: What IS the idea?

The ruling force is the wish: What is the *wanted* experience? And out of this idea, then, creation followed. So, what is the driving desire?

It is to have *different* experiences, watch from different viewpoints, play out different possibilities and different roles; to experience oneself as part of everything – and not in its totality.

We may think of this idea as a lengthy novel with a huge number of narrative strands, all happening in parallel but only readable individually. And regularly changing the characters in the plots.

This is exactly what's happening in the universe. The source, all-that-is, is constantly present (how else could it be) as what we call consciousness – but not to be confused with individual consciousness. In our individual experience, both are always present: Individual consciousness having the experience, and consciousness observing it. Whilst the experience can end at any moment, the consciousness is still there.

In other words, it is like a film which we're both viewing, and taking part in at the same time.

Let me reiterate: *Collective* consciousness is something different. Whilst in psychology it may ultimately point to interconnectedness and oneness, in sociology it mainly refers to shared ideas and values. We'll explore this in more depth when we look at ways to create a more loving, common experience of humanity.

The sixth level sets the parameters for our experience. If there was only singularity, of course, there would only be *one* – or one-ness. There cannot be any opposite. So, in order to *experience* itself, oneness needed to be broken up.

And as this is impossible by default (one is one, not two), the idea of time and space was introduced. A bit like a dream: We travel through different worlds, and it may feel never-ending. But eventually we always wake up.

The framework for this experience, which we call the universe, is then fine-tuned, and ideas are added, such as cycles, lifetimes, opposites, genders, taking on roles. And, of course, the opportunity that we completely identify with the role we temporarily assume, so we're entirely immersed in the experience. All this is powered by the foundation of creativity: *free will* (which we will examine in more detail later).

For the level of form, laws of physics, chemistry, energy (what we today know as "quantum physics") were established – as well as gravity and the ego, to keep the experiences in a certain place.

The next levels show how this plays out in detail. For now, we just need to repeat the idea behind the creation of the universe and let it sink in. This is the basis for any understanding and any potential change: We want to experience difference, we want to experience multitude, we want to experience individuality, we want to experience limitation.

And the most important aspect, because on the soul level, we know that all this is just an experience: there are NO LIMITATIONS in the experiences.

On the sixth level, there's no lack of love. Why should there be? The knowledge that all is connected is the key to everything.

The Fifth Level

The fifth level is where the experience starts. It's the creation of viewpoints – or of universal forces.

Here, the big forces dominating every experience were established: Exploration and freedom, power and dominance, creativity and pleasure, intimacy and belonging, trust and safety, knowledge and dedication, service and care.

These forces are neither good nor bad. They simply exist to gain experience. What we today perceive as the universe is essentially the playground of these forces.

Ground-breaking 20th-century psychologist Carl Gustav Jung was one of the first to identify how they play out in the everyday – and how they create a basis for psychological understanding of personality types. He realised that every person was driven by several – and often competing – forces, which he called *archetypes*.

As a way to gain a deeper insight into our own personality, these are a foundation of the Reiki Revolution, and will be examined in more depth in the next chapter.

On the fifth level, these forces also form entities representing their positive power. In the Abrahamic religions, Judaism, Christianity, and Islam, these archetypes are often referred to as the *Archangels*. They not only symbolise one or more of these forces, but can be called upon for help and guidance. (In Hinduism and Buddhism, the concept is similar, and they are respectively called Devas and Bodhisattvas.)

As they are, to a certain degree, separate entities, the Archangels also show that there's some fluidity between the fifth and the fourth level.

And the fifth level has had an addition for some time, too: *Ascended Masters*. These are previously incarnated individual beings who went through millennia of different lifetimes, and eventually began to understand the set-up of the universe so they were able to deeply re-connect with our origin. They're now able to add the experience of physical, individual incarnations to the universal forces. The Ascended Masters were the catalysts to the conceptual changes that we're able to continue today.

The more detailed examination of the idea of archetypes provided later on will start to shift these changes inside of us.

On the fifth level, there's no lack of love, either. Why should there be? The forces are just different ways to experience love.

The Fourth Level

The fourth level can be called the *soul level*, as here the individual souls are formed which then encounter the many different experiences the universe is designed for.

Often mistakenly referred to as "heaven" (though it surely feels like this compared to our physical existence), this is the level from which we enter a physical lifetime, and to where we're eventually returning.

It's a level with greater wisdom and overview than the physical – but where we also continue to develop and learn. Just as in the physical, we also learn in the spiritual realm, both through experiences and teachers.

There's a whole range of teachers at different levels of wisdom and awareness who then continue to guide us through an incarnation, but whom we sense in very different ways: There may be our grandmother, who primarily wants to send her love; there may be an old schoolteacher or neighbour, who sees the bigger picture and the theme in our lives and wants to help us if we lose track. Or we might even connect with the highest echelons: deeply experienced spiritual teachers and ascended masters.

Past-life regressions, research into near-death experiences, and intuition and mediumship allow us a better understanding of this level. It's unimaginably vast and has many different levels in itself. There are parts that surround individual planets and others from where you can swap between planets or galaxies.

There are "younger" and "older" souls: People who've had a few physical lifetimes, and those who've lived many. Our spiritual development isn't necessarily dependent on the number of lifetimes, but it always involves more than just a few. Those older souls, like in a school, have taken on the role of educating the younger ones and will discuss the experiences of their lifetimes after they return. Some of these souls may not incarnate again.

Though the fourth level is made up of individual souls, the surrounding aura – and eventual physical appearance – changes. With each incarnation, we may change our gender, our abilities, and our ethnicity and the traditions we're born into – which also has an effect on our personality in the spirit realm. We're aware of all our previous incarnations and see our experiences as a bigger picture – the lesson we intended to learn or the experience we wanted to explore – and continue to construct a bigger body of experience.

At this level, we also group together in *soul families*. In the physical realm, when we feel an unexpected attraction or familiarity with another person – an explicable pull beyond the physical – it's very likely that they're from the same soul family. We often incarnate together in changing roles, sometime just switching between parents and children.

On the fourth level also awaits something very unexpected for us: An enormous number of people whose only hope is *us*. They bank on us, rely on us, and indeed trust us; because only *we* can make the changes in the universe.

As odd as it sounds, only at the third level can these changes be instigated, because it's the end of the line of the soul level. Here, we have the most extreme experiences, and can therefore make the most extreme decisions and changes.

On the fourth level, there's still no lack of love. At least not in the beginning. It's about diversity in harmony.

The Third Level

The third level is our current experience: The level of form, the world as we know it. The experience takes on a physical shape – with all its limitations, challenges, and extraordinary potential...

The entrance to this level is nothing but a small-scale recreation of the beginning of the universe. After what usually is a warm, loving, caring, and safe nine months in our mother's womb, we're thrown out into the "real" world. And straight away, literally cut off.

So, our physical life, without exception, starts with a moment of fear. Severing the navel cord. We're expelled. Disconnected. Left on our own.

And it only gets worse: After this rite of passage, we're born with (near-) total amnesia, believing that this is our one and only life.

And if we do remember, if there are any remaining glimpses of our connectedness as a young child – which has been well documented – then over time, convention will override this. As a child, we're told we're making up stories, we're "fantasizing". Only what we can see with our physical eyes is real. And we come to believe that – and so our three-dimensional experience begins to take shape.

We cling on to our parents (if they're around), but eventually realise that they can't shield us from much. Not from chicken pox or colds, not from heartbreak when our nursery friends turn away, not from accidents, and not from the internal unease that starts to set in. Subconsciously, we find it irritating to be able to be only in one place at a time, and are frustrated by our physical limitations, which differ from person to person.

And talking about differences, we encounter different genders, intellectual capabilities, physical abilities, interests, tastes, different emotions. Even different languages, cultures, and skin colours.

There's difference wherever we look. What a magnificent set-up! What amazing opportunities to learn and experience!

And how incredible that, beyond these superficial differences, we're all connected. We're all souls. We're all connected to the same source. Only, we don't normally see it.

So, we're stuck in the division, and in the fight for survival and recognition. Because who are we if we're not recognised by others? The super-rich find it challenging to see meaning in life, the extremely poor struggle with pure physical survival. And of course, many of us have illnesses and disabilities we're born with.

This constant struggle is the foundation on which we build our society – and then wonder why it so often fails to work.

This isn't just a human challenge; being incarnated as an animal puts us in the same position. When I received my information about these levels, it was made clear that there's equal value in either incarnation.

And there's another problem, which turns out to be the worst: Given the amnesia at birth, from an early age, we view death as something scary, as irretrievable loss, rather than a transition or a coming-and-going between dimensions. If we *do* believe in life after death, it's often associated with judgement or punishment.

In either case, death is our primary source of fear which, over time, combines with karma, the energetic law that states action creates energy. An unpleasant action, therefore, ends up creating unpleasant energy. And we don't know how to turn this energy around.

However, we also experience love: Whenever we overcome the division, through physical or emotional attraction, family bonds, or shared interests, we can uncover love in many facets.

The Reiki Revolution is about making changes on the third level, un-creating karma, and opening up to more love.

On the third level, suddenly, there's a distinct lack of love. It's replaced by fear. And with extraordinary repercussions in the universe. Everything's connected, so it can be felt throughout.

The Second Level

The second level is the basis of organic life. We commonly call it nature: Soil, plants, trees, fungi, bacteria. Seeds, growth, composting; the concept of cycles and seasons.

The further the study of biology develops, the more the interconnectedness of all life is revealed.

Recent research of trees has established how they communicate underground, to a point where struggling specimen are allotted more nutrients from the ground. The role of fungi as communicators and connectors is only starting to be uncovered. The healing mechanisms in nature are at the heart of life's survival.

At this level, nature can adapt in a myriad of ways, and this provides the basis for our human existence. Even though the set-up is different, nature has feelings: The only way for consciousness to *experience*.

Against this background, the idea of *respect for nature* takes on rather a deeper meaning – and provides the cornerstone for the Reiki Revolution.

Much of nature has neither been researched nor understood – including the world of water. Although chemically counted as inorganic, it's not only the basis of organic life (and present in all living organisms), it provides also a habitat for life.

Once we feel the calming, cleansing, and peaceful effect of being in nature; realise its interconnectedness and mutual support; or, indeed, sense an energetic connection with it, we may come to the conclusion that love is at the very basis of nature.

The First Level

The first level is the level of matter. But even in matter is consciousness...how could it be any other way?

Even though the first level is the inorganic, it provides the basis for life: water and minerals. And not just on this planet – the entire physical universe exists only at this first level. The extraordinary images from the James Webb telescope are nothing but images of this level of existence – the platform for our three-dimensional experiences (and an experience of consciousness in itself). Just imagining the experience of the eruptive force in the building of new planets and galaxies can offer an idea of the enormity of the divine creative force, the seventh level.

As random as it may seem to us, there's perfect structure in the entire physical universe. Astrophysics, as well as astrology, reveals a sacred geometrical structure behind all that we experience here. A level more easily accessible to our understanding can be viewed in the range of the different magnetic capabilities of crystals.

Of course, this is not the only inhabited planet, and we may well spend other incarnations elsewhere. But rather than trying to relocate to the Mars in this lifetime, we need to sort out our lives here. Otherwise, the problems will stay the same. Everything else is nothing but a waste of resources and money.

The first level holds the awareness that everything is one. So, of course, by definition, the level is love.

The original meaning of the word "*Rei-Ki*" is the direct connection to the highest existence in the universe. The 7th level.

Please note that the seven levels of existence are only a model, so we can understand the concept. The reality is far more intricate and complex. But it provides a remarkable overview for our level of understanding – which has already been around since ancient times, and is even represented at the four-thousand-year-old temple in Karnak, Egypt, where in the inner temple is the representation of seven doors as the gateway to heaven.

For several hundred years, though, science and spirituality were viewed as opposites.

Religion – or spirituality – was preoccupied with the deep questions of meaning and ethics; science, with the physical functioning of the world.

But the two are not just interwoven, the two are the same. My guides have told me that my next book will cover a much more detailed understanding of this idea.

B. THE ARCHETYPES

The universal forces described above exist to create experiences from different angles. They do that by working together to create these experiences, but they're not somewhere "outside", in the universe; they work through us and within us. One might say they're a blueprint for the human experience. And for the myriad of *different* experiences.

Each person has different combinations of these universal forces within them, some extremely distinct and dominant, others lingering in the background. We're fascinatingly complex beings, yet no matter how much we learn and develop in a lifetime, the unique combination of forces remains the same.

But to a degree *every* force is within us. So, we need to learn how to live with them. Only once we've mastered this about ourselves can we accept the different mixes in another person as well.

The different forces really don't make it easy for us: Someone may, for instance, be dominant in the forces of love and safety – as well as in equal measures of the forces of exploration and power. Which force do we follow? It may well be that we feel pulled apart internally.

This is the reason why we often have such a turbulent inner life... We want peace, but we also want to explore; we want to be loved and accepted, but we also want to rule; we want to serve but we also want recognition; we want to learn but we also want to rest and play.

In fact, the conflict between these forces is the true source of any problem in the world – but only as long as we see them as competing. Why can't they *complement* each other?

If we find a way to approach them with this understanding – from the point of love rather than fear – our inner world can turn around. And, consequentially, the outer can, too.

Psychologist Carl Jung referred to the more challenging forces as the "shadow self". We try to hide them away or shield ourselves from them, until their influence becomes so powerful it destabilises us. We become a split personality.

The more we try to suppress these parts of us, the more we struggle, and feel hurt and internally harassed. It's therefore vital to understand that these forces are neither good nor bad. They're there for our experience. And our relationship with them changes from incarnation to incarnation.

It's up to us how we use these forces. The following exercise will help to change your perception.

There are many different categorisations, from Enneagram to Kabbalah, or simple "personality types", but I still feel that the following summary of archetypes, proposed by Jung, gives a particularly clear overview:

81

The Sage *– representing knowledge*

They want to find truth through Scientific research and self-reflection. Intelligence and wisdom are keywords, and lifelong learning through books and practical experience, as well as special interests and hobbies, fall into this category. Or it might mean simply asking again if an explanation doesn't make sense to us. For some, it's an everyday curiosity about life, others dedicate their whole life to a particular field of interest. Of course, another side to this persona may be the feeling of superiority.

The Innocent *– representing safety*

These people want to be happy and do things right. Feeling safe, trusting in the good in people, and being an optimist is one side of this force; the need for security, a safe home, and fear of something new or unexpected is the other.

The Explorer *– representing freedom*

This type seeks a more individually fulfilling life. Travel, openness, ambition, and exploration are key here. They struggle when they feel restricted.

The Ruler *– representing control*

They want to be in power and in control, but also look after others and create prosperity and security for them. Protection, influence, responsibility, and success are keywords. Of course, leadership can be used in both positive and negative ways.

The Creator – *representing innovation*

They want to realise a vision. Art, beauty, philosophy, creativity, and imagination are applicable. The idea is to do something unique.

The Caregiver – *representing service*

These just want to help others. Words such as generosity, compassion, kindness, and selflessness are key. But they may also feel responsible, even if events are out of their control.

The Magician – *representing power*

They want to understand the universe, then use this knowledge to create change. Vision, invention, and charisma are often found in this type, but healing and shamanism are also connected with them.

The Hero – *representing mastery*

These people want to make the world a better place, and shine in what they do. Keywords are courage and competence.

The Rebel – representing liberation

These want to overturn the status quo and overcome boundaries. Freedom, revolution, and equality are their descriptors. However, their methods can sometimes wander into the unlawful.

The Lover – *representing intimacy*

They want to be in a relationship – with people, work, or even places.

The Jester – *representing pleasure*

These types want to live in the moment and create joy, both for themselves and others. They love to entertain, tease, and play, but can easily get bored.

The Regular Person – *representing belonging*

These people want to be connected, and blend in without standing out. Solidity, participation, and realism are keywords.

Archetype Exercise

It's obvious that all these forces can be used in different ways, e.g.: "I'm the ruler, but I want to lead by example and inspiration, not by suppression and fear."

This exercise can give us more insight as to how we, ourselves, are structured – and how this can serve us (and others) in a positive way:

1. Read through the list of archetypes and take a moment to reflect how dominant this aspect is within you. Then select the three most dominant characteristics.

2. Read the description of each of the three again and ask yourself if you're using this force from a point of love or fear. It may well be that you find both directions applicable.

3. Now take a moment to think about how you can use these dominant personality traits only from a point of love instead of fear, from respect instead of anger, and abundance instead of scarcity.

Now let Reiki help you:

4. Connect to Reiki, place your hands, palms together, in front of your chest, and ask Reiki, "How can I use this force from a point of love?"

5. Then move your hands, still with the palms touching, to the point between your eyebrows – the third eye – and listen to the answer.

6. Then place your hands on your heart for a few moments and let this change register.

7. Do this for each dominant force individually, then end by thanking Reiki for the insight.

At some stage, you may want to use this exercise for each of the 12 archetypal forces, as they're all part of you.

It's entirely possible to use these forces with joy, happiness, understanding, love, acceptance, respect, and creativity. None of them need to be destructive. They're what we make of them.

By doing so, we change not just our own experience, but the entire universe.

Indeed, every exercise in this book will empower you more and more to make these changes.

C. KARMA AND FREE WILL

So, the universal – or archetypal – forces are one part of the problem. The way we deal with them is another – because we can use them *any way we like*.

The biblical allegory of Adam and Eve shows this vividly: They were told not to eat the fruit from the "forbidden" tree, the apple, but did, and were subsequently expelled from paradise. In a way, we're all expelled from paradise. Because we're individual beings, and paradise can only be felt in oneness.

The story really serves as an illustration of being separate from God. And of course, as discussed above, that's the whole idea of the universe: To experience what it feels like to be a *part* but not *all*.

In a way, the story personalises the experience of individualisation and of having a free will.

Because both Adam and Eve, could have said "no" to the 'temptation'. But they chose differently. And experienced the consequences of a "bad conscience".

This is what we're confronted with every single day. Only, it's not clear what God wants – or doesn't want us to do – because *there's no such direction*. We can do whatever we want. Because what we create is *only an experience*.

The idea of free will is one of the key principles behind the creation of the universe. And what a magnificent concept! It's in the DNA of every human being paired with consciousness. Consciousness is the observer; it experiences, but creation has free will to drive the experience in an unlimited number of directions, facets, and possibilities.

This starts at birth, even though there's initially, of course, a huge dependence on our parents. Our first experiences are a mix of free will combined with helplessness and the need for support. Our first trauma is created and continues through the rest of our incarnation. The idea of the all-knowing, supportive parents is at some stage overtaken by reality: We realise there are areas of our lives that are beyond their capabilities to support, and we start to experience their limitations.

We end up losing trust, and the dominant force of love is replaced by fear and separation (the latter having started at birth, created by the trauma of separation from the physical connection with our mother). We feel more and more helpless and dependent, but as adults we often don't have anyone we can depend on.

Free will is now paired with fear.

We also have an almost insatiable drive to explore, and our free will takes us further and further along this route. Especially as teenagers and young adults, this can be incredibly exciting.

We feel that the whole world is ours and we have unlimited possibilities – until we start noticing there are obstacles, too.

And we make decisions that may, in hindsight, turn out to be unwise. We might do things that seem good for us but are not helpful for other people. Or we do the opposite: suppress our free will and do what others want us to do – and feel unhappy. Increasingly, we realise that our actions almost take on a life of their own, because they have consequences. Everything is energy. Therefore, with every action (indeed, even with every thought) we create a new energetic constellation.

This is called karma: The energetic footprint we leave. It's impossible to escape this – but up to us whether we create positive or negative karma. And, of course, these experiences build up over many incarnations, and we continue to create more karma. The whole world is now a web of karma, created through every single incarnation that ever occurred.

In between incarnations, we may get to see the bigger picture, like a theme or learning curve, and decide that next time we want to – or we may need to – look at experiences we've had from a different perspective. So, in addition to free will, we're confronted with the results of our free-will actions.

There's no judgement in any of this, only experience – even though we often build up feelings of guilt and shame. Because we realise that our actions lead us to the opposite of what our soul longs for: Happiness. Love. Oneness.

Incarnation after incarnation, in unlimited variations and iterations, we reach the point where we find the game exhausting. We may have an opportunity to take part in a past life regression, and finally understand that our husband in a previous life may be our son or daughter in this one. So, no matter what the husband has done – and we may sense that there's been violence, misunderstanding, a toxic family atmosphere – we might now experience the opposite. Or we may still work through elements of that trauma, through repetition.

Let's summarise: *The state of the world is the result of a toxic mix – a combination of free will, karma, and fear.*

We're in a vicious circle. With each incarnation, we search for love, fulfillment, and happiness. Yet our experience of it is only fleeting, and compromised. Most of the time, we experience the opposite.

So, is it impossible to find what we're longing for in this temporary set-up of ever-changing constellations in the universe?

I believe it is. We can use our free will and decide to change.

We need to change the rules: We still want to play, explore, experience... but not *everything*, or at any cost.

The toxic mix can be dissolved. The next part shows how.

Part 2

THE INNER
REVOLUTION

Let's get to the actual program. Each exercise will have an immediate effect on your well-being – and step-by-step, you will feel lighter, happier, and more connected. And then, life becomes more meaningful.

There are three phases:

1. *Realisation* – discovering who we really are
2. *Change* – finding a different perception
3. *Application* – bringing change into our everyday lives

Please take your time doing the exercises, and only read the next one once the current one is completed.

Here are two helpful ideas before we start.

Help is at hand

EMERGENCY REIKI

Some of the following exercises might feel more challenging than others, and unhappy memories may surface, or you may find that current reality hits you straight in the face.

I suppose we all have own ways of reacting to difficult news: Some people freeze for a while or remain shocked in disbelief, whilst others find their mind all over the place, or feel they must jump into action.

Anger is often the most immediate reaction (Why hasn't this event been prevented? Why is this happening again? And why to me?). This is often followed by *worry* (What shall I do? How do I cope? What comes next?).

Whenever you struggle, please use this very simple exercise, which will make an immediate difference.

Over the years, I've developed a very simple mechanism that I now put into action when confronted with a challenge. I call it **Emergency Reiki:**

I simply connect to Reiki, place my hands on my chest at the level of my heart, and let the energy do its job. Often, I'm so confused by a situation that I don't have any intention about what I'm hoping to achieve – but this really doesn't matter.

I just leave my hands there until I feel better, no matter whether it takes two minutes or twenty.

This technique isn't just meant for big disasters. The first time I used it was when I'd burned a curry meant as a special treat for my family. After mum tasted it, and confirmed that it was inedible, I gave in to the obvious, and was about to go to a supermarket to buy a ready-made version. But it just wouldn't have been the same, so, to deal with my frustration and calm me down for a moment, I sat down on my sofa and gave myself Reiki. After 15 minutes or so I felt better and went to the kitchen to throw the curry away.

Something prompted me, though, to check it one last time. And, to my great surprise, I could only taste a very slight hint of it being burnt. Could it be – somehow – that my Reiki self-treatment had something to do with it? I now bombarded the curry with Reiki, and twenty minutes later it was restored back to perfection.

Of course, I told everyone at the dining table what had happened, and they were doubly careful in checking the curry: Nobody could detect any bitter aftertaste.

The more we use this technique, the more it will come as a natural reaction in difficult situations.

Emergency Reiki Exercise

This is one of the simplest exercises in the entire book. But in difficult times, what we need the most is simplicity...

1. Whatever worries you, makes you angry, or you find difficult to deal with today – think about it for a moment, acknowledge it's there.

2. Have a look at the clock to check the time.

3. Now, set your intention to connect to Reiki and **place your hands on your chest, above your heart**. The hands can be on top of each other or next to each other.

4. Sense the loving warmth of Reiki and focus on the physical sensation and area where your hand is.

5. Leave your hands there until you feel better, more relaxed, more energetic again.

6. Check the time once more, to see how long the treatment took. Sometimes, you may find that three or five minutes is enough; at other times, to your surprise, half an hour might have passed.

Or you can use the most basic version:

> Connect to Reiki, place your hands on your heart, and leave them there until you feel a positive change.

To get used to the practice, **throughout today**, whenever something worries you (or you simply could use a Reiki boost), apply "Emergency Reiki" for a moment.

The Foundation
ALLOWING HAPPINESS

In ancient Rome, politicians came up with a very smart concept - *Panem e circensis* - which translates as "bread and circuses". As long as you keep people fed and entertained, they're not looking for change.

Today, have we really moved on from this?

Of course, we need to eat, have a roof above our head, and an income. Possibly also we need outer security, police, and some structure. But entertainment? Interestingly, that's exactly the same trick we're playing with ourselves at present: Television, streaming channels, music on earphones, social media. Most people are constantly bombarding themselves with entertainment. Or we dream of a getaway, a holiday, or pour our passion into sports.

To a large degree, we do this to distract ourselves from something else. Our inner unhappiness.

Do these activities really make us happy? Of course not. As soon as the distraction is over, we're back to square one.

Some people are good at finding at least *some* balance. They'd call themselves "content". But...happy?

Are we asking for too much? Do we actually *deserve* happiness? Happiness every day?

If you go inside now, while pondering these questions, you'll very likely feel some resistance. Do I really deserve complete happiness?

Struggling to find a wholehearted "yes", a subconscious programme pops into action: We don't allow ourselves to be happy.

Happiness is a wonderful state. Or rather, happiness would *be* a wonderful state.

I don't know anyone who doesn't want to be happy.

We try to catch it, we try to hold on to it, we're chasing it. And yet, it rarely lasts longer than for a few moments.

We may even form the idea that our own happiness inevitably comes at the expense of others'. We think out of scarcity rather than abundance. We think from a three-dimensional identity rather than as being spirits in a body.

At some stage, we try something new: We start looking for meaning and spirituality, so we can argue there's more to life than superficial happiness – we give up on the things that make us happy in the name of spirituality.

But happiness isn't superficial. It's essential.

In fact, spirituality doesn't work without happiness. And true happiness is not without meaning.

The best version of ourselves is a happy one.

And your happiness also affects other people. Have you ever sat next to a deeply unhappy person and noticed how it affects you? Or, on the other hand, how contagious a happy person can be?

You're allowed to be happy! Why should the universe not want you to be happy?

The entire Reiki Revolution programme is designed to get beyond our erroneous self-identification with shame, guilt, fear, or unworthiness, and open us more and more to happiness as a daily companion.

Happiness is the foundation of spirituality.

And it brings more energy, creativity, and health!

GASSHO – this is the first exercise in which we're using *Gassho*. It's a Japanese word and simply means "bringing the hands together". Whenever we use this expression, gently place your hands, palm against palm, in front of your chest at the level of the heart. In the West, this is often referred to as the "prayer position", but in Reiki it's just meant as a starting point for concentration.

Happiness Exercise

To start, let's take a moment to reflect what makes us (or *would* make us) *happy*.

NOTE: Please read through the exercise once or twice before you actually start.

For this exercise, you'll need three different-coloured pens:

1. Please take a piece of paper and write your name in the centre using a colour of your choice: This represents *you* – at the centre of your universe.

2. **Now,** choose a second colour and write around your name everything in your life you're happy about. **Take your time** – you may want to pause in-between and reflect on all these beautiful things, no matter whether they're something material, emotional, intellectual, or in your awareness. Some may have to do with other people.

3. **Next**, take the third pen and write in the remaining free space everything you'd like to make you happy – or happier. Any goals, dreams, desires. Anything you feel is missing. Be honest – and don't be shy! Really take your time to jot down everything you'd like to add to your life. It may even overlap with your previous list – something that already makes you partially happy but could be better.

If you wish, you can rank the goals: Circle those that are really important, underline the ones that are *quite* important, and leave the others as they are.

This is an important exercise – it will give you more clarity. If you struggle to name what's missing in your life, take a breath and ask Reiki to help you focus.

And now, let's take action:

1. **Look** at the "happy universe" you've created and read through everything *you want to achieve, and* everything *that's missing at present.*

2. **Then** place your hands in Gassho (the prayer position), close your eyes, and connect to Reiki. When you feel the connection, ask Reiki to help you achieve the changes you wish for. You might simply say, "Please Reiki, please universe, help me reach my goals and bring the change in a way that's right for me."

3. **Now** comes the most important step: Letting go. You've asked for help, now the universe has started to be in charge... **Just accept that.**

4. **Finally**, return to your "happy universe" and read through everything that's already in place.

5. **Connect** to Reiki again and take a moment to thank the universe. Really feel the gratitude.

Please **take your time to complete this process**. If you're too busy in the morning, leave it until later in the day – just make sure it'll be done at some stage today.

You've taken an extremely important step, or, rather, two: Realising what *is* – and asking for help. **Now Reiki has taken over.**

While the universe works in the background, we can begin working on ourselves, to become more open and receptive...

A.

REALISATION

The first series of exercises is designed to help us make the most important realisation in our lives: I am a spirit in a body, I am an eternal being. And I am connected to everything.

The understanding might already be there – but it needs to deeply resonate. It needs to become an awareness. And this can only be achieved through experience.

Realisation 1

I AM CONNECTED

A friend of mine is an analyst. She confessed recently that she was really good at taking things apart, probing every single aspect, dismantling everything. But then she struggles to put them back together. It seems that this is something we all do: We take things apart and then we're lost looking at the fragments and can't see the whole anymore. The Reiki Revolution is exactly the opposite: It starts with the whole, the bigger picture, our connection. Every topic and exercise is related to the totality of all things – and to our connection with it.

Let's start with the connection...

In March 1922, a man walked up Mount Kurama, not far from the Japanese city of Kyoto where he'd spent the previous three years. His name was Mikao Usui, and he went to the mountain because he was fed up with life (which may sound familiar during these difficult times).

For several years, everything had been going wrong. First, he lost his business and went bankrupt, then he struggled with the rituals and hierarchy in the monasteries he'd joined searching for a deeper meaning, and had to leave.

He might have ended his life on this mountain, had it not been for a strange and sudden experience after three weeks of fasting and meditating.

Today, Mikao Usui is famous for the creation of the universally known energy healing system that we call Reiki. Except, for him, its physical healing effects were a secondary effect.

His main focus wasn't on the application – but on the source.

After 21 days on the mountain, he suddenly saw light and felt a strong connection to high-vibrational energy. Or, in more philosophical terms, to "a higher power". What, before, had been only theory for him suddenly became experiential. He had proof.

Only accidentally did he then become aware that this connection also meant he had healing powers which he could use for himself and others.

No matter how we use Reiki in our daily lives, this connection is always the basis. And it's this "higher power" that will bring the change we're currently seeking.

Today's exercise, therefore, is designed to help you come to the same realisation Mikao Usui did a hundred years ago...

Connection Exercise

This exercise is actually pretty advanced – and I often find that we need to be in the right headspace for it. Therefore, if it doesn't completely work on your first attempt, try it again. And please read all the steps before you start...

1. Connect to Reiki and choose an area to place your hands on your body. (Alternatively, you can place your hands in Gassho – bringing the palms together and holding them in front of your chest. Or you can give Reiki to an object, e.g., placing your hands around a plant, or an item you're holding).

2. Focus on the sensation in your hands, feel the flow of Reiki, and observe what's happening now.

3. After a few moments, try to **trace the Reiki back to where it's flowing from.** Begin at your hands, then up your arms, into your torso, and so on... Quite likely, at some stage your awareness will extend beyond your body.

4. Don't visualise; just observe where your intuition takes you.

5. Now, **feel the connection in both directions** – the area of your body or the item receiving it, and its source. Observe how this feels for a while.

6. Next, maintain your **focus on the source**. Stay there and take your time exploring it. Really let the power of this connection sink in.

7. Thank Reiki and come back into the here-and-now.

You may want to do this for five or ten minutes, but it's also OK to just quickly dip into this exercise. At some stage, you may feel that you don't just observe the connection, but actually merge with the energy.

For the rest of the day, remind yourself from time to time of this connection. Whether you're doing the dishes, working on the accounts, looking after your children, speaking to your colleagues, or watching TV – the connection's always there. The more you do it, the more you'll get used to this as the foundation of your life.

Realisation 2

I AM ENERGY

Around the time I started teaching Reiki, I came across a small book that described how to see auras. I was so fascinated that I tried it out as soon as I was home – and it worked!

Ever since, it's become the first exercise in my Reiki 1 courses, as it's such an amazing icebreaker – and remarkable proof that there's more to us than just the physical body.

Today, we'll use this simple method to reassure us of our multi-dimensional existence (which we'll have a deeper look at tomorrow).

I tend to find that the vast majority of people are able to see the innermost layer of an aura, as it's at its densest close to the body. Just like the bright line around the body in the picture above, it normally stretches to a depth of about 1 inch (2cm) around the body. Most people detect it as a lighter or brighter field, and many can also see something like a pencil-drawn line where it ends.

It's quite rare to be able to see further layers or colours of the auric field, so don't worry if you can't.

Everyone – and everything – has an aura: A while ago I woke up one morning and saw the aura of the antique dressing table in my bedroom.

The aura can, of course, also be felt. We often feel if somebody is upset or excited simply by sensing it – which means we're picking it up from their energy field.

Near my mother's new home near Berlin is a park with a famous oak tree called the "thousand-year-old oak". It's assumed that its real age is not quite as far advanced as that, but it's still several hundred years old. When we recently walked into the field where it stands, we had to stop about 50 metres away because the energy was so overwhelming. It was both peaceful and powerful.

Aura Exercises

1. Seeing your Aura

1. Stand in front of a mirror.

2. Look at your face.

3. Now move your gaze slightly above or sideways, so you can see what's behind your head.

4. See if you can detect a brighter field or small line surrounding your head.

5. Think vividly of something sad and see whether the energy field changes.

6. Then think vividly of something positive and see whether the energy field changes again.

2. Give Reiki to your energy field

1. Connect to Reiki and choose an area to place your hands – close to your body but keeping them at a distance.

2. Slowly bring your hands towards your body until you can feel your energy field.

3. Let Reiki flow for a few minutes, with the intention that it fills your aura.

4. Pay attention to the difference in how you feel.

5. Thank Reiki, and come back into the here-and-now.

3. See other Auras

1. Look at another person from a distance of a few metres. If you do it at home, it's easier if they stand about a foot in front of a plain wall.

2. First, look at their face.

3. Then, move your gaze slightly above or sideways, so you're focussing on what's behind their head.

4. See if you can detect a brighter field or small line surrounding their head, shoulders, or entire body.

5. Notice whether it changes your perception of the person, now you can see that there's more to them than their physical body.

6. Do the same with a tree outside and see if you can detect the aura around its trunk and branches.

4. Feel an Aura

1. Stand behind another person (it's easier if they're seated) and ask if it's OK to touch their aura.

2. Stretch out your arms sideways, then slowly bring the hands towards the person's head.

3. Pay attention to any sensations in your hands – signals that you're touching the person's aura.

4. Stop there and feel the connection.

You can also do the same with a tree: Stand a foot in front of the tree, set your intention to connect with its aura, then bring your hands forward, with your palms facing the tree, and slowly move towards it until you feel the aura. Stay there for a moment. Don't forget to thank the tree for sharing its energy with you!

So, what does this all mean? Simply put, we're more, much more, than our body! Over the next few exercises, it will become increasingly clear that we're not a body with a spiritual connection, but a spirit *in* a body.

Realisation 3

I AM MULTI-DIMENSIONAL

Being multi-dimensional can be as exciting a realisation as it is confusing. How do we align the different parts?

The answer is, by opening up to both of these facets of ourselves. Then we become a naturally integrated person.

As explained in Part 1 of this book, the system of Reiki focusses on three main energy centres - the *Tanden*. This concept doesn't invalidate the popular idea of chakras – the lower Tanden (just below the navel) can be seen embracing the lower three chakras, the upper Tanden (between the eyebrows) the upper three, and the central Tanden correlates with the heart chakra. Their vibrational levels correspond with the Reiki symbols.

To locate each centre, place your hands, one on top of the other, in front of the three points and, one by one, try to feel the energy.

In the exercises to come, we'll go through the Tanden centres, open them, and begin to align them naturally with their associated frequencies.

Even though the same concept is at the heart of many other Eastern spiritual traditions, the main (and often only) focus is usually placed on the lower Tanden. What sets Reiki apart is that it makes all the frequencies available to everyone, not just a select few.

The first Tanden – which in Japanese culture is often called the *hara* – is the centre of our physical energy, representing the material level of form. Although we're an incarnated spirit, we're IN A BODY. The body is the most extraordinary tool, enabling us to have all the experiences we can, in an incarnation.

Many martial arts traditions (and the Samurai) focus on building strength in this energy centre. Unlike muscle strength, this is more energetic strength, with its endurance, resilience and performance, and strengthening the immune system. But it's also connected to everything that physically exists at the level of form.

Using the **Power Symbol** is a way to access this level of energy, and is often used to promote physical healing and boost physical energy.

The following exercises show a number of techniques to help **build up strength for our existence at the level of form**.

Hara Exercises

1. Hara Breathing (Joshin Kokyu-Ho)

IMPORTANT: Please don't use deep abdominal breathing if you're pregnant or have any physical issues associated with your abdominal region. Normal breathing with the same intention will be enough.

Joshin Kokyu-Ho is deep abdominal breathing. If you practise yoga, it'll be familiar to you; if not, it'll feel strange. But you'll soon get used to it! An amazing technique, it's the opposite of what we're used to. Rather than breathing into our chest, we breathe into our *belly*.

Between the stomach and lungs, there's a muscle called the diaphragm. It's attached to both the stomach and lungs, which means that the movement of one affects the other. We use this in this exercise, moving the stomach out, and therefore pulling the lungs down. This allows us to breathe into the full depth of the lungs.

1. Sit on a chair, or cross-legged on the floor, keeping your spine straight.

2. Place your hands in the *Gassho position* and connect to Reiki. If you've learned Reiki 2, draw the Power Symbol and repeat its mantra.

3. Then bring your hands to your lap or knees and let them rest there, palms up. (You can also place them on your belly to support and feel the *Hara*.)

4. Set the intention to *breathe in Reiki energy*.

5. Breathe in through your nose, deeply into the lowest part of your lungs. As you use your diaphragm to pull the air in, let your stomach expand outwards. Concentrate on the sensation of the air coming in through your nostrils and filling your lungs. Once the

lower parts of your lungs have been filled, you'll notice that your diaphragm relaxes slightly.

6. Carry on filling the middle and upper parts of your lungs – all in one deep inhalation. It can take up to eight seconds for an in-breath. But don't worry if it doesn't. Everyone is different.

7. On the out-breath, use your stomach as a pump and, starting at the bottom, gently squeeze out the air until your lungs are completely empty. The in- and out- breath should be the same length. Intend only to breathe out the stale air, whilst building up Reiki in your body.

8. Continue breathing in deeply, intending or visualising that you're breathing in Reiki.

9. After a few minutes, you can go further and, while breathing out, intend or visualise that the energy is expanding through your whole body and even beyond, into your aura.

10. You can continue for up to 15 minutes if you wish. Be sure to stop if you feel dizzy; you can extend the time gradually as you continue your practice.

11. Finish by placing your hands in Gassho and thank Reiki.

12. Remain seated for a moment and notice how you feel. More energised? More present? Has any discomfort or pain eased?

2. Self-Treatment of the Hara

Connect to Reiki, draw the Power Symbol if you learned it, place your hands on your Hara (about two fingers' width below the navel), and give yourself a treatment with the intention of building up physical strength, endurance, and your immune system.

Pay attention to how your strength gradually builds up.

3. Chanting the Kotodama

Unknown to most, there's another way of accessing this vibrational level - chanting. Our research with water showed that it's surprisingly effective. Each Reiki symbol has an accompanying *Kotodama* (literal meaning: "Spirit of the word").

If you learned Reiki 2 at the ReikiScience Academy or another school that teaches this method, you can just connect to Reiki, close your eyes, and spend a few minutes chanting the Kotodama associated with the Power Symbol.

However, even listening to a recording will do the trick. Thirty minutes of recorded chanting improved the quality of a bottle of mineral water, as our research with water has shown.

You can access recordings of Kotodama for all the symbols through www.thereikirevolution.com.

Realisation 4

I AM SPIRIT

When I visited Mount Kurama on my first ever day in Kyoto, I had an unexpected encounter with a statue. It represented **Amida Nyorai**, a Buddhist deity that appears in a number of different traditions – but especially in Pure Land Buddhism, the tradition in which Mikao Usui was raised. The Saihoji temple in Tokyo, his burial grounds, as well as the temple located in his birthplace, Taniai, also belong to this tradition.

The symbolic figure is part of an intricate mythological story, but the idea behind it is relatively simple: Amida Nyorai represents the idea that we can *connect directly to the spiritual realm.*

The huge statue I'm referring to can be found in a sub-temple on Mount Kurama. When you stand in front of it, you can only see the upper half. To see the entire figure, you need to crawl under a small, wooden bridge and kneel down. From this position, you can see directly into the statue's eyes. Then, an extraordinary secret is revealed: Amida Nyorai's right hand has a rope attached to it, with the other end dangling down. It's actually an invitation to the visitor to hold on to the rope and feel a direct connection to "the above". I remember being really surprised at what a powerful connection this symbolic act invoked.

The Japanese symbol for Amida Nyorai is the inspiration behind the Harmony Symbol in the system of Reiki. It's not an exact copy, but has a very similar meaning: Connecting to spiritual realms, to guidance, intuition, harmony and balance.

It's directly related to the Upper Tanden, the brow chakra. This, unsurprisingly, is often also called the "third eye" as it allows us to "see" and sense what's beyond the reach of our physical eyes.

These exercises will open up the third eye powerfully – and over the following exercises, we'll then work to deepen our intuition...

Third-Eye Exercises

1. Become aware of the connection

1. Take a moment to listen inside and see if you can feel a connection to the spiritual realms. If you wish, focus on your brow chakra.

2. Then connect to Reiki, and feel the connection in your hands and your whole being.

3. Now, once again, listen inside and see if you can feel a connection to the spiritual realms, and if anything has changed.

2. Self-Treatment of the Upper Tanden

Connect to Reiki; if you've been taught it, also draw the Harmony Symbol, then place your hands on your "third eye" and give yourself a treatment with the intention to open up to deeper spiritual insight. This should last for at least 10 or 15 minutes.

Keep your attention at the point between your eyebrows and note anything that comes up: Colours, images, ideas, or memories.

3. Chanting the Kotodama

You can also spend a few minutes chanting the Kotodama for the Harmony Symbol – or listening to a recording (see exercise 3).

Once again, keep your attention on the point between your eyebrows and note anything that comes up: Colours, images, ideas, or memories.

Realisation 5

I HAVE HELP

The more we use Reiki, the more we open up to intuition and guidance. Often, we sense what's going on in another person's life and may even give them advice. Much more difficult, though, is to use intuition for oneself. It can easily be confused with wishful thinking. But there are amazing techniques that can be learned, and the more we practice, the more we feel this guidance in our everyday lives.

Receiving guidance can work in very different ways, but I tend to find that everybody can open up to it. The technique of *Reiji-Ho* surprises me every time I use it.

Intuition Exercises

1. Open up your body through physical exercise

Physical tension can be an obstacle to intuitive insight – it keeps us in the body. Therefore, please take a moment and do some gentle stretching.

2. Loosen up tension around the third eye

Now, place your index fingers on your third eye and gently massage the tension away. Smooth the skin around the eyes and on your forehead but don't apply too much pressure.

3. Give yourself an intuitive Reiki treatment using *Reiji-Ho* (which translates as "guided by spirit")

1. Sit comfortably, place your hands in Gassho in front of your heart chakra, and connect to Reiki.

2. Now keep your hands there and ask Reiki, "Where shall I place my hands?"

3. Move your hands (still in Gassho) slowly to your third eye and listen to your intuition. It may be a word, an image, or just a general sense of knowing where to go. Then, place your hands according to your intuition. (If you're not sure, just follow this process again or simply decide where you're going to place your hands without engaging your rational mind.)

4. From time to time, ask Reiki, "Am I still in the right spot or shall I move somewhere else?" If you feel you should move somewhere else, follow this intuition; if you feel you should stay, just do so. I often stay in just one position for an entire treatment.

5. When you finish, place your hands in Gassho, and ask, "Why was I drawn to these areas?" You might get an interesting answer. If you're not sure, just accept that Reiki will have guided you anyway. You may get a sudden insight later.

4. Give an intuitive Reiki treatment to somebody else

1. Stand next to the person, place your hands in Gassho in front of your heart chakra, and connect to Reiki.

2. Now, keep your hands there and ask Reiki, "Where shall I place my hands?"

3. Move your hands (still in Gassho) slowly to your third eye and listen to your intuition. It may be a word, an image, or just a general sense of knowing where to go. Then place your hands according to your intuition. (If you're not sure, just follow this process again, or simply decide where to place your hands without thinking about it.)

4. From time to time, after 5 - 10 minutes in one place, ask Reiki, "Am I still in the right spot or shall I move somewhere else?" If you feel you should move somewhere else, follow this intuition; if you feel you should stay as you are, just do so. You may well stay in one position for an entire treatment.

5. Place your hands in Gassho, thank Reiki, and finish the treatment.

There's nothing more reassuring than getting confirmation of our intuition from somebody else, so make sure to get some detailed feedback. However, it sometimes takes a while for the recipient to make sense of a treatment, so don't be disappointed if the feedback is not offered straight away.

Other means of guidance...

We all stop from time to time, look back at what we've just seen, and wonder whether it was a sign: An image, a recurring number, a logo or marketing text – or even a scene we watch on TV. We feel it somehow wants to guide us about a question we have or a situation we're in. But how do we know it actually *is* a sign? I tend to find it's about two things: Our gut feeling – and learning by doing.

5. Ask Reiki for inspiration

Connect to Reiki and ask for inspiration, then go to your bookshelf, pick any book that draws your attention (even if you've read it many times before), and open it at random. Just read a paragraph or sentence that sticks out to you and see what it means in relation to your current situation – or as inspiration for the day.

6. Be open to signs

If something unexpectedly catches your attention and resonates, just pause for a moment and see if you can find a deeper meaning...

If your eyes are caught by the logo of "Mothercare", for example, maybe you should phone your mum and check on her. Or, if she's already back in the spirit realm, she may want to say "hello", and show her love and care.

If you see an old-fashioned Peugeot, it may remind you that today is the birthday of your old friend who moved to France.

7. Pay attention to numbers

Years ago, I read about the meaning of recurring numbers, such as 111 or 3.33pm... Ever since then, my basic guide to their meaning has been as follows:

- 111 stands for "don't worry, it'll have a good outcome".
- 222 means, "this is an important lesson for you".
- 333 is "the Masters are helping".
- 444 indicates "the Angels are helping".
- 555 means "big changes are about to happen".
- 666 tells you "don't worry about money".
- 777 means "congratulations, well done!".
- 888 foretells that "big changes are imminent".
- 999 means that "a period is coming to an end, new beginnings are on the way".

You may find that, over time, certain number combinations have a particular meaning just for you, which is also fine.

You might also spot a meaning in birth dates or other numbers with a special connection to you. When I was on my first research trip to Japan, there was a moment when I felt rather lost. I was in a taxi to a temple for a morning meditation, pondering over some new information I'd found, and suddenly the bus in front stopped and I could read its number plate. It had several Japanese characters, and in-between, a number: 1710 – my birthday, 17 October, in Western Arabic numerals I took this as confirmation that I might be on the right track. But I was still doubtful. What if it were a coincidence?

When I arrived at my destination, I simply couldn't believe the price shown on the taxi's meter: 1710 Yen. I finally accepted the sign.

Please, don't actively search for the numbers to pop up – they'll appear when you need them.

8. The simplest guidance of all

If you have to make a decision you're unsure about, you can simply write the options on small, separate pieces of paper, fold them, and place them in your hands. Then connect to Reiki, ask for guidance for the right decision, shake your hands, holding the different options, and pick one. You might want to include a paper saying, "none of these options", as well.

Realisation 6

I CAN TRUST

Spirituality relies on *trust*. If we can't do this, it's nothing but wishful thinking.

But trust is pretty hard work. We've all had so many disappointments in our lives, and often trust has been abused and shattered. As a result, naturally, we've built a wall around us and decided to be cautious rather than fully trusting.

I felt the same way when I started with Reiki. How could I possibly trust an "energy healing system"? What did it do? How did it work? Why was it so difficult to explain it?

It took many years to entirely trust it (and I've detailed this journey in my recent book).

The main factor that kept me going with Reiki was that **it simply worked**. No matter what I used it for, there were results. And this is indeed why it's so popular all over the world. No belief is needed, not even trust; we can just experience it: Firstly, the physical sensation of our "healing hands", and secondly, the results.

The images of the water experiments (which can be found on www.thereikirevolution.com) are a powerful reminder: They show the effect on the crystallisation of the minerals in water after Reiki. Swiss tap water improved from decent-quality tap water to entry-level spring water (suggesting that its quality had reverted back to that of water from a natural source). Given that our body mass consists of approximately 80% water, it's easy to conclude that Reiki will have a similarly beneficial effect on our physical bodies.

Internalising that Reiki really works – with scientific proof and in measurable, physical ways – also has an additional effect: We begin to trust. And, as the word "Reiki" means spiritual – or universal – energy, this means **we can start to trust more in spiritual – or universal –** *guidance*.

Both, consciously and sub-consciously, we realise we're connected to a higher power.

Therefore, please don't underestimate the effect of these simple exercises.

Exercises to trust

1. Remember your experiences with Reiki

If you've already learned Reiki, you'll have had many experiences, and very likely life-changing ones. It may have started with the first time you actually felt something during a Reiki treatment, or, possibly, when you experienced physical healing for yourself and others. And it may also have brought some profound changes in your life, either in your awareness or, indeed, your circumstances.

So, please take a piece of paper now and write down as many of these as you can remember – at least 10.

Then place your hands in Gassho and thank Reiki.

2. The Reiki Water Test

Fill two clean glasses with tap water, then put one aside and give Reiki to the other glass for 10 minutes (or longer if you prefer). Simply connect to Reiki, then place your hands on the glass or slightly away from it, and let Reiki flow. If you've learned Reiki 2, you can also use the Power or any other symbol for this exercise.

Once you've finished, take a sip from both glasses and taste the difference.

You could also use a jug or bottle instead of the glass and do a "Reiki water-tasting exercise with family and friends.

3. Give yourself a Reiki treatment

Now sit or lie down for 15 - 30 minutes and give yourself Reiki. You can do a complete self-treatment with different hand positions or simply focus your hands on one area, e.g., your heart, solar plexus, or stomach.

Be sure to pay close attention to the sensations you feel (physical, emotional, spiritual, or as thoughts or guidance).

While you give yourself Reiki, try to sense the healing effect it's having on your body – just like the changes to the water you've just tasted. You might even get a visual image in your head...

The more we use Reiki, the more we begin to trust. And sometimes it's good to remind ourselves of what we (and Reiki) have already achieved.

Realisation 7

I AM LOVE

When our third eye begins to open – when we start trusting our intuition, receiving guidance, messages and signs from the universe – we feel more and more aligned.

I tend to find that most people think, "this is it", we've found our way of connecting with the universe and with who we really are – there's no way this can be topped!

Well, there actually is, and this is the mind-blowing result of the water tests I did in Switzerland, so let me repeat it:

Using the Power Symbol and focussing on physical healing brought a huge improvement in the quality of water and showed that the physicality of the entire sample of the water was permeated with Reiki.

Using the Harmony Symbol, using our connection to guidance and intuition, then showed crystallisation mainly on the outer edge of the sample – pointing towards something higher, or outside of our physicality.

But the biggest surprise came with the results of the use of the Connection Symbol: these crystals were the biggest of all. And not only that, but they also actually started to touch, overlap, and grow towards each other. As a result, the water quality was the best of all the samples.

So, the highest power we can access isn't the power of physical strength and perfection, and not the power of spiritual understanding, but the power of the heart. The power of love, connection, and oneness. And this is what we're tapping into now: the following exercises are centred around the heart chakra.

These findings are completely in line with recent scientific research showing that much more information is moving from the heart to the brain, rather than the other way around.

The belief that humans are brain-steered, brain-centred and brain-controlled, that we have to think in order to create, is plain wrong. We have to *feel*, and we have to *love* for the act of creating. Because WE *ARE* LOVE.

Heart Exercises

The first step, today, is to open our hearts – or heart chakra – more. Please pay attention to how these exercises make you feel – about yourself, about others, and about the universe. After all, it's not possible to keep the feeling of love to ourselves. It's all about connection.

130

1. Connect to your Soul

Take a deep breath, bring your awareness to your heart, and sense how you feel... This is the centre of your true self. This is your soul: YOU ARE LOVE.

Do this exercise throughout the day, every few hours or so, and become more and more aware of its importance. It was a huge discovery for me that the centre of love can actually be localised in our body. Which is why it's so important to understand the energetic set-up of it.

2. Self-Treatment of the Middle Tanden (which I prefer to call "Central Tanden")

1. Connect to Reiki.

2. If you've learned it, draw the Connection Symbol.

3. Now, place your hands on the centre of your chest at the level of your heart (I tend to place one hand on top of the other) and give yourself a treatment, with the intention to open up your heart chakra and connect to your soul.

4. Keep your hands there for at least 10 or 15 minutes.

You may want to check whether you feel any difference placing your hands in the centre of your chest or slightly to the left, on the actual physical heart.

3. Repeat the truth

Throughout the day, repeat to yourself "I AM LOVE" and sense how this feels.

4. Chanting the Kotodama

You can also spend a few minutes chanting the Kotodama for the Connection Symbol – or listening to a recording (see exercise 3).

Keep your attention on your heart and sense how you feel.

B.

CHANGE

Much of what we see around us is based on perception – and there are many different angles to this. Even the seemingly obvious – facts apparently set in stone – can take on different meanings or interpretations, as our perspective is always influenced by its relationship to our memories. Even the past, the number one factor holding us back, can change in retrospect, when we shift our perspective.

It's very rare, therefore, that we live fully in the present moment and explore it with openness. Yet, real change is only possible in the present moment.

German philosopher Gottfried Leibniz once said, "The place of the other is the true perspective."

Following the exercise of self-realisation, we'll now explore the changes that can follow.

Change 1

LOOK FROM A HIGHER PERSPECTIVE

Almost twenty years ago, I read in a book the most puzzling thing I'd ever heard: The idea that our life is not the only one – but one of many.

It didn't fit in with the beliefs I'd held all my life – but the more I thought about it, the more it made sense.

Reiki then turned this philosophical idea into something more tangible. The energy and experiences I started to open up to left me in no doubt that life indeed goes on after death.

I love the idea of stepping through a door – *birth* – into an incarnation, having all the experiences we encounter and then, one day, leaving it through another door – *passing* – only to be reconnected with this higher reality.

My experiences when I use Reiki are confirmation that even while we're "down here", we're always also connected to the spiritual realm. We're a SPIRIT IN A BODY.

And the irony of life is that we spend so much time searching for it – until we eventually re-connect to this eternal truth.

Therefore, now, I'd like to explore a bit more about how this awareness can change our understanding in quite surprising ways; which, of course, makes sense when we acknowledge that we might experience more than one life in a body. We suddenly look at life in a different way. We begin to wonder what we're supposed to experience and learn *this* time round.

Perspective Exercises

1. Repeat the truth

Sit down for a few minutes and repeat to yourself: "I'm a spirit in a body." Keep saying it over and over.

Sometimes we just need to hear the truth.

Now, let Reiki help you make more sense of the experience of this incarnation:

2. Think of a problem you've recently encountered

1. It doesn't matter whether it's one that's now resolved or something you're still struggling with.

2. Then connect to Reiki and ask for help to see it from a higher perspective.

3. Now, try to see this problem from the perspective of looking down on it as a spiritual being: What were you meant to learn? What were you meant to experience?

3. Go further back and try to understand as many challenges as you're able to confront at this moment

Then connect to Reiki and ask for help to see them, one by one, from a higher perspective. Just listen inside and wait for the answers.

4. Let Reiki heal you

Give yourself a few minutes of Reiki, especially if the insights are unexpected or upsetting, and allow it to give you calm, peace, love, and healing.

5. Change your perception

For the rest of the day, whenever you see somebody, remind yourself that they're ALSO a spirit in a body, walking around the earth plane in one of their many incarnations. They may look very different, be another gender or have a different skin colour... but they may have looked just like you in a previous incarnation. And the other way round.

Change 2

DISCOVER YOUR HIDDEN TALENTS

A few years after I first came across the idea of reincarnation, I read an analogy that really made sense to me: It suggested that, before we decide to jump into our next incarnation, we pack a little backpack with everything we need.

Having trained so many students over the years, I'm always amazed at how different the content of our backpacks is. I've found people with the most extraordinary variety of talents – sometimes blatantly obvious, at other times so hidden that it either takes a long period of searching or they become only aware of them through a sudden challenge they rise up to.

I gradually realised that it's deeply satisfying to use our talents – rather than trying to imitate others and do what isn't right for us. Therefore, today I'd like you to do a bit of soul-searching for your talents.

Please don't be shy – your list isn't meant to be read by anyone but yourself. It's not about boasting; this is about realising what we've been given. And, of course, using it.

Talents can be twofold: those we've learned and perfected, and those we were born with. You're welcome to write down both, but I'd suggest focussing on those which come naturally to you (e.g., being musical, good at ball games, having a good memory, being a good listener, effortlessly connecting with people, having a great eye for art or fashion, being academic or naturally organised, and so on...).

Talent Exercise

This exercise isn't as predictable as you might think. Following the steps below could lead to some surprise revelations...

1. Write down your talents

Once again, take a piece of paper, or use your notebook, and **write down all the talents you have**. No matter how big or small, write down everything you feel is special about yourself. You might want to go through different aspects of your life (intellectual, practical, social, spiritual, etc...).

2. Go a bit deeper

Now, take a moment to **remember what other people say about your talents**. You'll have received comments and compliments regularly from others about what they think you're particularly good at. Take some time to note them down.

3. Ask Reiki

Finally, place your hands in Gassho, connect to Reiki, and ask the universe, **"What are my biggest talents from the viewpoint of the universe?"**

Add these to your list.

4. Are you using your gifts?

Now, again connecting to Reiki, ask, **"How should I use them?"**

Do you think you're using your talents enough? Are some being wasted? How would you feel if you used them more?

To finish, take a moment to **thank the universe for what you've been given**.

I'm sure that recognising your amazing array of talents will lead to some interesting new insights over the course of the day...

Change 3

ACCEPT YOURSELF

We've now gone through several exercises which helped us look deeper into our extraordinary, multi-dimensional self.

There's so much potential to strive, to be successful, and to live life to the fullest!

And yet, in our everyday lives, we often hit a wall, struggle with so many tasks, and wish we had more abilities in so many areas. There are times when we're on the brink of despair: No matter how hard we try, we have to admit that there are things other people can do better. There are many things that others excel in – in fact, we might not even be able to do them at all.

Our body may not be *able* enough, or we lack the creative or intellectual mind frame. And yet, those talents would be so helpful and make our lives so much easier.

In the previous exercise, we looked at all our special abilities: Everything we put into our backpack in readiness for this incarnation. It's a lot – and it's amazing to become aware of them!

But why did we also leave so many things out? Wouldn't it have been much easier if we packed a bit more? Or different things? Maybe a better memory for foreign languages, better math skills, a natural ability to use social media, or a basic knack for cooking?

And why did we pack other things that are so challenging for us? Which hinder us in our daily lives, which bother us, or which weigh us down? Such as physical problems, the weird family we were born into, or deep-rooted anxiety?

It's perfectly OK to ask all these questions. In fact, it would be scary if we didn't! But...even pondering the idea that it might have been OURSELVES who chose the items for the backpack can be the start of a very different outlook. If we accept that we're here for a reason, these obstacles will also have a reason.

Acceptance Exercise

It's therefore essential to try to understand why we've brought these difficulties into our lives. This may not be the most enjoyable of exercises, but it could well turn out to be one of the most rewarding...

1. Take a moment to sit down, get a piece of paper and **write down the things you've been struggling with**. It may be a few things...or an entire list.

2. Then place your hands in Gassho and **connect to Reiki.**

3. Close your eyes and **ask Reiki the following questions:**

- Why did I bring these challenges with me?
- What are they for?
- What can I learn from them?
- And – what have I *already* learned from them?

Step by step, go through the entire list and see **what insights you receive and what they allow you to learn**. I'm talking about abilities here, not experiences. But of course, your abilities – or lack of them – also led to particular experiences, so they may also come into play.

4. To finish, please place your hands in Gassho once more and **thank Reiki for this deeper understanding.**

Change 4

FORGIVE YOURSELF

In Germany, there's a saying: "A clear conscience is the best pillow to rest on." But who *does* have a good conscience? At least an entirely good conscience?

The last exercise marked a big step: Accepting that we have shortcomings. And that they're an integral part of our human experience. After all, spirit is what we are, anyway...

Once we accept ourselves as a person with faults, life gets so much easier. It doesn't mean we shouldn't strive to improve, to learn, to develop – but we also begin to accept that we all have different talents and can't always do everything to the same quality as everyone else.

Sometimes, though, we fall short of what we wish we'd done – and our lack of abilities isn't the problem. Rather, we did or said something we could easily have handled differently. And that we later regret.

Some of these regrets may be so overwhelming that they turn into an all-consuming feeling of guilt. We constantly ask ourselves, "Why did I say this? Why did I do this? Why didn't I see this? How on earth could I have been so careless or negligent?"

Sometimes, we have the chance to say sorry or make up for it; often, not. Either the opportunity never comes, or it's too late.

We're then left with this dreadful feeling of having failed. Often, this turns into anger – towards the situation, the world, and ourselves. It's the worst place we can possibly be in.

And in our inability to deal with the guilt, we close ourselves off. We become compartmentalised – we're not whole anymore, and need deep healing. We need to learn to forgive ourselves.

Yesterday, we accepted that we have shortcomings in our abilities – today, we need to realise that we also have shortcomings in our behaviours. And accept it as part of our development.

No matter what we've done, whether we said something wrong, didn't pay attention, angered somebody, caused an accident, made somebody's life miserable – it's all in the past. We may have made a terrible mistake, we might simply have been careless, or we may even, for whatever reason, have been intentional in our actions. But, again, it's all past.

It's *our* decision whether we become a product of our past or whether we can learn from it and move on.

Reiki is all about change, *positive* change, and it's completely non-judgemental. The universe doesn't ask whether we're worthy of receiving help and healing. It's open to everyone without conditions (although it may lead to a change of behaviour afterwards, but that's a different consideration).

Indeed, I'm certain that Reiki would be an amazing tool for working with prison inmates (and heard a while ago that there are already projects going on).

Reiki also helps free us from the prison we've built around us through guilt. Just imagine how Mikao Usui must have felt after becoming bankrupt – owing money lent to him in good faith; not being able to provide for his family. Wouldn't he constantly have been thinking of what he could've done better?

This was the situation in which he found himself when he discovered Reiki. And it's also when he realised that he was allowed to forgive himself. Because the universe had already forgiven him.

Forgiveness, really, is accepting that things can go majorly wrong in an incarnation on the level of form, but it doesn't affect who we really are: A soul, an eternal being having a temporary experience in the limited shape of a human.

For Mikao Usui, the connection to Reiki was proof of this. And an experience of forgiveness.

On the soul level, forgiveness is the default setting.

Self-Forgiveness Exercise

The following can be done one problem at a time, or you may feel you want to go through everything in one go.

1. Take a moment of **deep honesty** and think about something you've done at some stage in your life that really bothers you. You might be surprised – it could even be something from your childhood.

2. Really **feel the problem** and acknowledge how it still affects you.

3. Now, **connect to Reiki and ask for help**.

4. Ask Reiki to help you **realise** that, beyond that experience, you're still a spirit in a body. **Become aware** of what you've learned from this event, and how you changed afterwards. Or, how you can change now.

5. Then ask Reiki to help you forgive yourself and say out loud: **"I forgive myself."**

6. Place your hands on your heart chakra and **feel the love and forgiveness of the universe**. Let Reiki flow for as long as you need it.

7. Place your hands in Gassho, **thank Reiki**, and feel the relief.

Whenever you think of the problem again in the future, remind yourself that it's now firmly in the past.

But if you feel you couldn't let go completely, then please join the 'club'. Self-forgiveness is one of the hardest tasks ever! It may take some time, but increasing our awareness of its momentous impact means we're already halfway there.

Please take this as the start of a journey, and continue working on it! Forgive yourself, because you are already forgiven.

Change 5

FORGIVE OTHERS

Forgiveness is such a misunderstood word; you might even be tempted to call it old-fashioned. Why do we forgive? Because we have to? Because otherwise we're the ones not forgiven? Because our religion tells us to? Or because we know that without forgiveness, we'll keep being held back?

There may be truth in all of this, but ultimately, what *is* forgiveness?

Forgiveness, really, is understanding. Realising that there may have been a mistake or misunderstanding, that there may have been different viewpoints. In many cases, this might do the trick. But what if what happened was life-changing? How can we forgive something truly horrific?

What we really need to understand is that whatever happened has been an *experience* – with, possibly, disastrous consequences, for ourselves or for other people.

But it has a beginning and an end. And it hasn't harmed our soul.

A misguided person, someone who may not be aware they're a spiritual being, a person full of fear, frustration and anger, may have carried out the act that has been so far-reaching for us. If we want to mitigate the effects, to move on, we need to forgive. We need to acknowledge that it's nothing but an experience.

When we practise *self*-forgiveness, it's not just for ourselves. If we struggle to forgive ourselves, we tend to struggle to forgive others as well.

There may be one, two or several people, or maybe even institutions, around you, where you're struggling to move on from challenging experiences you've had with them. And quite rightly so – because what they've done has caused incredible difficulties! It may even have been so traumatic that it changed the course of your entire life.

But it also caused another problem: It's keeping you in the past. Sometimes partially, sometimes completely. It distracts you from the present moment, from experiencing joy, happiness, and fulfilment. And it may well keep you from moving to a brighter future.

You're reading this book because you really want to move forward. This is why today we need to look at forgiving others. This can be a very big challenge – but let Reiki support you with this...

Forgiveness Exercise

Please read the following steps a few times before you start.

1. Take your time to sense inside and become aware of what people have done to you that you haven't been able to let go. It might be something surprisingly small; it could be something huge. There will likely be several issues, so you may want to write them down. You can also ask Reiki to help you find and remember these unresolved experiences – some may be hidden deep within your subconscious.

2. One by one, really *feel* each problem and acknowledge how it still affects you. It'll likely be a rather unpleasant reminder, but it's important to bring them up for healing.

3. Then, for each issue, connect to Reiki and **ask it to help you to forgive and move on**.

4. You might also ask Reiki to help you realise that, beyond that experience, you're still a spirit in a body. **And that spirit cannot be harmed.**

5. Now, each time, say out loud, **"I forgive this person. I forgive this situation. I realise it was nothing but a really difficult experience on the level of form."**

6. Listen inside once more and see if you get an idea of what you might also have learned from this experience.

7. In the end (depending how intense it's been, either after each memory or once you've gone through

them all), place your hands over your heart chakra and **feel the love, forgiveness, and freedom of the universe**. Let Reiki flow for as long as you need.

8. Then place your hands in Gassho, thank Reiki, and feel the relief.

And a suggestion:

If you struggle with this task, you may find it useful to ask Reiki to help you see the problem from the other person's perspective. **Was their action perhaps the result of a mistake, a misunderstanding, or was it born out of fear or anger?** Could it be that they're also struggling with this memory?

Is action needed?

If revisiting an experience inspires you to take action to resolve it or deal with it in a certain way, now you have the momentum to do so! It's possible to do both at the same time – forgive AND take action.

I'm well aware that for some people, hugely traumatic experiences may come up – and you'll really want to keep them in the past, rather than revisiting them. The problem is, they'll keep triggering us if we don't address them at some stage. So please give the exercise a go... When it becomes too difficult, please stop for a moment and give yourself "Emergency Reiki" – just connect to Reiki and place your hands on your heart.

Once again, you may find that forgiveness isn't always a single act but a journey.

Change 6

ACCEPT OTHERS

Over the past decade, I've had the privilege of meeting thousands of wonderful people who came to my courses – and was always gobsmacked to realise how many incredible and unique talents people had.

So... how do we deal with OTHER people and THEIR uniqueness? Do you find it easy to accept them, even if their interests, abilities, and lifestyles are the polar opposite to yours?

Preparing for this next topic, I was given three keywords to explore or, rather, to apply:

ACCEPTANCE - RESPECT - LOVE

Acceptance of the other person, no matter how different, and difficult, to understand they might be – because they're also a **human being**.

Respect for the other person – because they're also a **spirit in a body**.

Love for the other person – because they're not really *another* person. On a soul level, we're connected. Essentially, they're just a different expression of **ourselves**.

Acceptance Exercise

1. Start with a specific person or situation

1. Take a moment to reflect on the ideas of acceptance, respect, and love – and hold each word in your heart.

2. Now, choose a person you know. Think of them, their characteristics and their lifestyle, and say the following silently in your mind: "**I accept you. I respect you. I love you.**"

3. If you struggle to really mean it, ask Reiki to help you.

4. Sense inside how you feel.

2. Let Reiki choose the person

1. Next, connect to Reiki and ask for intuition as to another person to pick.

2. Then repeat the first exercise: Think of this person, their characteristics, and their lifestyle, and say the following silently in your mind: "**I accept you. I respect you. I love you.**"

3. If you struggle to really mean it, ask Reiki to help you.

4. Sense inside how you feel.

5. Place your hands in Gassho and thank Reiki.

3. Extend it to everyone

1. Whenever, you meet someone today, say silently in your mind: "**I accept you. I respect you. I love you.**"

2. Again, if you struggle to really mean it, ask Reiki to help you.

3. Afterwards, sense how you feel inside.

Change 7

LETTING GO OF ANGER

A while ago, I tried to make some changes to my website... and failed hopelessly. I wasn't even able to upload a new logo.

A couple more frustrating experiences completed the picture. What a day! There were several moments where I must have looked like the angry emoji. And no, I didn't feel particularly happy.

But, of course, my emotions didn't change anything.

Interestingly, Mikao Usui made the famous five Reiki principles one of his core teachings. They start with the sentence: "Just for today, do not be angry." Usui obviously identified anger as one of the main blockages to spiritual development and connection.

When we listen inside and sense how we feel when we're angry, it's not a pleasant experience. We may even struggle to sense what's going on at all, because we're so angry. It blocks us completely.

Consequently, this makes us react in unhelpful and unexpected ways.

When we do something out of anger, we tend to regret it eventually – often immediately. We act differently from how we'd normally behave, often in the exact opposite way we would've reacted with the gift of hindsight.

This doesn't mean we should put ourselves down for being angry. In fact, anger is a normal, natural reaction to something unforeseen, something unaccceptablc, to a broken promise, or when things go wrong repeatedly.

It's normal for anger to come up. But anger is a reaction, not a solution.

And this is exactly what Mikao Usui wanted us to know: Become aware of your anger. Then look for ways to turn this energy into positive change. Suppression of anger makes us sick; changing it heals us.

Sometimes we might be quite rightly angry because something's simply unacceptable. Then we need to address that, of course – but, again, not from a position of anger, but of meaningful change.

Anger is often prompted by situations that remind us of similar situations in the past. It takes us back to our childhood, to disappointments, being side-lined, overlooked, not listened to, or denied something we really wanted. As a result, what we're feeling isn't a reaction to the actual situation, but to something we've been holding on to for a long time, and now project onto a similar situation.

If we're angry because we're disappointed, we might ask ourselves what we'd expected an outcome to be, and how we came to this expectation. Now that things have turned out differently, there's no way forward other than adapting and dealing with it.

If the situation's too overwhelming, the most important thing is to take a step back – and take a few deep breaths. The emotion of anger releases a set of chemicals in the brain that are flushed out of the body in 90 seconds. In other words, any anger we hold on to for longer than 90 seconds is a matter of (possibly subconscious) choice.

So, give it some time. And give it Reiki.

Connect to Reiki, feel it deeply in your heart, remember who you are: A spiritual being having an (unpleasant) experience.

But there's also a deeper meaning to it – even if it's only to remind you to let go, accept, forgive, and move on.

When we look at the state of the world (our own, small world, as well as the planet), it's obvious, scarily, that many of the problems were created out of anger.

Reiki is all about high-vibrational energy – and anger is the opposite. Low-vibrational energy is designed to keep our focus on the three-dimensional world. It effectively prevents us from realising who we really are.

Anger Exercises

1. Identify the anger and let go

1. Connect to Reiki

2. Take a few deep breaths, sense inside, and see if you feel angry. Note what you're angry about. Be honest. There may be one problem, or a lot of different ones, big and small.

3. Now repeat, "Just for today, do not be angry, do not be angry, do not be angry", again and again. Observe what happens: There may be more anger coming up, you may become aware of the original problems that caused your anger, and you may even start a process of moving on. Don't judge yourself; it's perfectly OK and normal to feel anger.

4. Then place your hands in Gassho and ask Reiki to help you. Next, place your hands on your heart, feel the connection and allow Reiki to work through the anger. If it gets more intense initially, just accept it. The process of letting deeply rooted anger surface can be painful.

5. Let Reiki flow until you feel better and the anger subsides. Forgive the people involved (whether it's yourself or others).

2. See it from a higher perspective

This is a repeat of an exercise we did previously. It shows that all these practices can be applied to different situations:

1. Feel your anger about a certain situation.

2. Then connect to Reiki and ask for help to see it from a higher perspective.

3. Now, try to see this problem from the perspective of looking down on it as a spiritual being: Why did this arise? What's behind it? Was there maybe a misunderstanding? Is it possible that other people see it differently? What can you learn from it? What could the other person or persons involved have learned from it?

4. Thank Reiki for the insight.

3. Transform the energy

In some cases, you may find that your anger is entirely justified. Something in your life or the world is not acceptable and it's simply not right.

Anger is, then, a wholly normal reaction, and might even serve to alert us to an issue. It can also teach us compassion, as we can then empathise with another person who's being mistreated. But the anger does not solve the problem. Therefore: TAKE ACTION!

Step into the power of being a spiritual being and do what you feel guided to do.

Connect to Reiki and ask what you can do to address and to change the problem.

Turn anger into wise action.

4. Throughout the day

Throughout the day – and indeed, in the future – whenever you get angry, take the following steps:

1. Take a deep breath and let the initial anger go.

2. Connect to Reiki and react as a spiritual being.

3. If you struggle, place your hands on your heart and give yourself "Emergency Reiki".

Change 8

LETTING GO OF FEAR

How often do most of us feel truly free? Like a huge burden has just fallen from our shoulders?

There was a reason why Mikao Usui began the Reiki principles with "do not be angry" and "do not worry". Again, they're not meant to tell us off, but to remind us that these two emotions often stand between us and, well, everything else: Other people, happiness, and our spiritual awareness and development.

Freedom from anger and worry is the hallmark of higher spiritual realms. In other words, both emotions are clearly connected with the three-dimensional world.

But, of course, we live in the physical realm, and it's natural to have these emotions. Everybody does. And yet, everybody also suffers from them.

So, what Mikao Usui really wanted was to invite us to explore what it's like to reduce this unhelpful influence over our lives. Let's therefore have a look at our worries today.

Are you worried at present? Then join the club! Don't put yourself down for it. Just try a few simple ideas to ease or let go of the worries...

Fear Exercises

To start with, take a moment and be really honest: What are you worried about at present? Are there several different problems? Is it more like an ongoing theme? Are they small problems or do they look unsurmountable?

Let Reiki help you...

As we're all different, try the following techniques and see which one works best for you. You might be surprised to find that you end up using different methods for the various kinds of worries you have..

I'd suggest addressing one problem at a time. And if you spend most of your day dealing with all your worries, why not? It will be worth it!

Technique 1: **Using your breath**

1. Set your intention to let go of your worry or worries.

2. Deeply breathe in, then make your exhalation twice as long. Visualise or intend that every exhalation carries your worries away...

3. You may find it's more powerful to breathe out through your mouth. Listen to the sound of each exhalation – it may be quite loud, almost rattling in the beginning, and slowly getting calmer.

4. Connect to Reiki and place your hands on your chest to calm and recharge.

5. Thank Reiki.

Technique 2: **Sending Reiki to the situation**

1. Become clear on your worries and focus your attention on them.

2. Connect to Reiki and set your intention to send it to the situation (no matter whether it's in the present moment or the future). If you've learned Reiki 2, you can also use the Connection symbol.

3. Send Reiki until you feel more at ease – and listen to your intuition.

4. You may get an idea about the situation or simply feel calmer, knowing that you've invited Reiki to help.

5. This can take anything between five and 15 minutes.

6. Finish by thanking Reiki.

Technique 3: **Give it to Reiki**

1. Connect to Reiki and set your intention that Reiki will bring it to the right conclusion.

2. This process can be rather quick. Just be sure to remind yourself that you've given it to the universe...

3. Finish by thanking Reiki.

Technique 4: **Auto-Hypnosis**

I did this exercise for the first time almost ten years ago, when I went through a particularly bad patch of "everything coming all at once". I'd intended to go to the gym as a distraction and to focus on other things, but was so worried I couldn't face going inside. So, I sat down in a chair in the lobby, closed my eyes, and just repeated the Reiki Principles for 20 minutes. In the end, I saw all the problems as individual and solvable, rather than one enormous mountain to climb.

1. Connect to Reiki.

2. Close your eyes and repeat the Reiki Principle over and over: "Just for today, do not worry."

3. No intention, no visualisation – just repeat this, and observe what happens.

4. This exercise may take a while, and don't be surprised if your worries seem to get worse at first. Just continue, and you should end up floating above the things that worry you.

5. Again, finish by thanking Reiki.

Technique 5: **Emergency Reiki**

If all fails, and you're so worried that you really can't think straight anymore, use "Emergency Reiki".

1. Connect to Reiki.

2. Place your hands on your chest and let Reiki do the rest.

3. Once you're calmer, you can try one of the methods above...

And finally, use any of the exercises we've done already to remind yourself that you're a spirit in a body. Look at the problem from this perspective. Ask your guides for help and guidance.

Change 9

GRATITUDE

Working on this topic made me realise how often I take things for granted: The hot cheese croissant and cafe latte I had this morning; the wonderful conversations with my family over Christmas; the crisp, fresh air during an afternoon walk...

The more I started thinking, the more ideas I came up with. And the happier I felt.

So, let's make today GRATITUDE DAY, spending time actively counting our blessings. And doing what I so often forget: *voicing it and actually saying "thank you". Not just to people, but to the universe, to the SOURCE.*

It took me several years to understand why Mikao Usui made a Reiki Principle of *"Just for today, be grateful"*. Initially, I thought it was simply a *nice idea* to say "thank you" (and probably more of a Japanese custom). But there's so much more to it: it's *very powerful*! Gratitude's all about energy, raising our vibration, and aligning with the universe.

Gratitude Exercise

This exercise has two parts, a short one in the morning, and one for later in the day.

1. The good old-fashioned gratitude list

1. Take a moment to listen inside and sense how you feel.

2. Get a notebook or piece of paper (in fact, you may find it useful to collect all the notes you've made working through this book and revisit them again at the end of the month), then sit down for a moment and write down a minimum of **10 things you're grateful for**. A good friend suggested this exercise again recently, and I found I didn't want to stop once I got going.

3. Spend a while considering all the things you've written down.

4. Place your hands in Gassho and just say, "Thank you, universe!"

5. Listen inside again and sense how you feel now.

2. Cultivating gratitude

Now, just go about your normal day. Only, with a little bit more awareness:

What's happening to me today? Do I have the use of a bicycle, bus, a train, or a car?

If so, say *"thank you"* for the opportunity.

Do you get an idea, an intuition, or have a "chance" encounter?

If so, say *"thank you!"*.

Do you have the opportunity to go shopping, listen to some nice music, or watch an interesting movie? Again, if so, just say "thank you".

Pay attention to everything positive happening to you – and say *"thank you"* every time.

Initially, you may overdo it a bit. However, practising gratitude isn't meant to hinder us, but simply to help us realise and appreciate the abundance of daily miracles we encounter.

You may even go a step further, asking: Where's all this from? Where are WE from?

You may then also thank the universe for the connection you feel, for the awareness it's allowing you to experience – and eventually, even, for the not-so-pleasant experiences that can help us learn and develop.

Whenever you remember or voice your gratitude, be sure to sense how you feel inside. Increasingly, gratitude will shift from an exercise to a habit.

Change 10

MINDFULNESS

For the past decade, mindfulness has become a hot topic. Bookstores have filled entire shelves about this subject, popular for its stress-reduction abilities without conflicting with any religious beliefs, while not being as demanding as meditation.

But beyond its blockbuster success, there's amazing depth to mindfulness. Most spiritual traditions, especially Eastern ones, remind us that the present moment is the only one that exists. We can't have a spiritual experience in the past, nor in the future. It's only ever in the NOW.

However, there are two versions of *now*, which is often misunderstood. There's the current, fleeting *now* (e.g., I'm completely present, watching a sunset, following its changing colours as it seemingly sinks into the ocean until it moves out of my sight) and the eternal *now* (feeling at one with everything, connected to the universe, and realising that outside eternity, everything's just an experience).

Even though the first is fleeting, it's the gateway to the latter; suddenly, a deeper awareness opens up.

In a way, every Reiki treatment is a meditation in itself, and there are often moments when we become aware of the eternal NOW: the everlasting presence.

I tend to find that the gratitude exercises are a great way to practice mindfulness – and many of the other exercises we've already done also help us to become more present.

But let's take this to a deeper level, and spend an entire day focussing on the present moment. Below are my suggestions.

Mindfulness Exercises

1. Start the day mindfully

If this email reaches you in time for the start of your day, see if you can do everything a bit more mindfully. When you shower, be in the present moment, really paying attention to what you're doing – the experience of warm (or cold) running water on your skin; brushing your teeth; savouring every sip of your coffee (or whatever you prefer in the morning).

2. Continue this throughout the day

Whenever you remember, be fully present in the moment: When you're walking, feel your feet on the ground; when you do the dishes, pay attention to every step of the process; when you speak to somebody, be fully present and really feel the connection with them.

169

3. Watch the movement and stillness in water

At some stage during the day, fill a glass or bowl with water and make it move by dropping a pebble in it or stirring it. Then, watch how the water settles. If you're lucky enough to live near a stream or lake, take a stick and stir up the ground below the water, then watch the sediment settle again. As the water becomes clearer and calmer, become aware of how your mind follows.

4. Do a simple breathing meditation

Sit quietly for a few minutes, close your eyes and bring your awareness to your breathing. Simply pay attention to the regularity of your breath, whether it's fast or slow, deep or shallow, and feel the air entering and leaving your nostrils. Everything is OK. Just observe, and let the breath connect you deeply with the present moment.

After a few minutes, begin to even out your breath, making the exhalation the same length as the inhalation. Don't think, just breathe.

If any thoughts wander into your mind, allow them to be there. Observe them without attaching to them, and then let them move on. I often visualise placing them in a cloud and letting them float away. Then return to focussing on your breath.

The mediation can last for anything from five to 20 minutes, or even longer. If you worry about time-keeping, you can set a timer to alert you when the time is up. This way, you can fully focus on the meditation.

5. Focus on your Reiki hands

Finally, at some stage of the day, connect to Reiki, keep your hands in Gassho, and focus on the sensation in your palms. Again, take your time and see if you experience a deeper connection.

Apart from the morning routine, the above exercises can be done in whatever order suits you.

Before you go to bed, please take a moment to reflect on whether the practices brought about any changes to your wellbeing.

Change 11

SELF-LOVE

OK...we're now much closer to a degree of self-acceptance, of self-understanding. Even of self-forgiveness. But self-*love*?

As fashionable as this word has become, what does it actually mean? In most contexts, it's connected with self-worth and self-care – and has even been included in the marketing of some beauty products.

Even though this is an important aspect – not neglecting ourselves while we look after others and *allowing* ourselves enough time to do this – there's a much deeper meaning behind it: self-love is really about *being* yourself, and about experiencing the love you hold inside.

Self-love means realising you ARE love. When you *are* love, then you don't just love others; you love yourself, and you become a beacon of love in this world.

A lack of self-love, on the other hand, can have disastrous consequences. It may turn into subconscious self-loathing, and even self-harm. Self-love means having inner peace, stability, connection. And with it, we also attract more love from others. All we need to know is where to find it.

Self-love Exercise

This exercise is extraordinarily important. And as with so many exercises, we need to repeat it continually, to really let it resonate.

1. **Connect to Reiki** and ask for help to open your heart and feel the love that you are.

2. Then **place your hands on your heart**, one on top of the other.

3. **Feel the love**, become one with it.

4. After a moment, **allow it to expand** into your entire body and beyond, into your aura.

5. Stay with this experience for as long as you wish.

6. Finish by thanking Reiki.

For the rest of the day, remind yourself of the love inside. Before you do or say anything, feel the love. Accept, respect, and love yourself. And then act and react towards others as this self-loving person.

C.

APPLICATION

From self-realisation, through the changes it brings, we've now arrived at the application phase – a stage that'll last for the rest of our lives. Therefore, the following exercises are just a starting point; the level of change you've already reached will offer many surprising opportunities.

The key is the awareness that we're not just interacting with "other people" but with other "spirits in a body".

Application 1 –

CONNECT AND UNDERSTAND

Moments when we feel deeply connected – or in fact *one* – with other people or even the whole universe, are truly extraordinary. They're glimpses of eternal truth.

But oneness can also be a challenge. Because we can't choose who we're one with.

Of course, in everyday life, we're given the choice of who we want to connect more closely with, and who we prefer to keep at a distance. Most of us have a few people who we'd be quite happy to meet as rarely as possible, or even never again.

Oneness, at a universal level, however, includes everyone and everything. It's simply how the universe is set up: As an outer experience of diversity, and an inner truth of oneness.

The more we open up to this existential truth, the more we connect with our own heart and our own truth.

When I tried the following exercise at a retreat for the first time, I became very aware of how difficult it can be – sensing a connection with a person we really (and possibly quite rightly) dislike. And yet, the feedback was so overwhelming it was clear it would become a cornerstone of this program now.

Deep Understanding Exercise

1. Connect with a loved one

1. To start with, think of a person you really like.

2. Then connect with Reiki and set your intention to deeply connect with this person. If you've learned Reiki 2, draw the Connection symbol to deepen this experience. This isn't meant as a Reiki treatment, so you don't need the other person's consent.

3. Take a few minutes to deeply feel the connection – the oneness – with this person, and see if you can really understand them with your heart.

4. Finish by thanking Reiki.

2. Connect with someone you don't like very much

Now comes the challenge:

1. Think of a person you don't really like. You might simply not feel very close to them, you might find them awkward – or you might deeply dislike them, to a point that you'd do almost anything to avoid them.

2. Then connect to Reiki and set your intention to deeply connect with this person now. Again, if you've learned Reiki 2, draw the Connection symbol to deepen this experience.

3. Take a few minutes to deeply feel the connection – the oneness – with this person and see if, with an open heart, you can understand them better,

discover aspects of them you haven't previously seen, or get an idea *why* they're so difficult.

4. Now, set your intention to disconnect from this person – if needed, you can clap your hands to end this exercise.

5. Finish by placing your hands on your heart to give yourself a few minutes of Reiki.

Do you feel that meeting them again would be different now?

Application 2

LIVING FROM THE HEART

The following exercises are much more gentle – but certainly no less powerful. They're an incredible reminder that, by opening our heart, *everything* can change.

I learned the fundamentals of these exercises from a voice coach – but rather than focussing on the effect they have on our speaking, what really amazed me was the effect on my perception.

The three exercises here are just examples, and the principle can be applied in a variety of situations.

Heart Exercises

1. Greeting from the heart

1. To start, either ask a family member or friend to join you for a quick exercise – or try it alone.

2. Then stand in front of them (or imagine somebody in front of you) and say something along the lines of: "Hello, good morning!" or "Hello, nice to see you!"

3. Now bring your awareness to your heart, and say exactly the same again – only, this time **directly from the heart.**

4. Notice the difference.

2. Speaking from the heart

When you have a conversation today, no matter whether on the phone or in-person, connect to your heart before you begin. Then **speak, feeling that everything's coming directly from the heart.**

3. Listening from the heart

In the same conversation – or any other – try also to **listen** to the other person not just with your mind but also **with your heart**.

Even if it's just the exchange of a few pleasantries at the supermarket checkout – do it from your heart.

Application 3

EVERYDAY KINDNESS

The final of the Reiki principles, *Be Kind to Others*, is all about action.

A friend of mine, Dr. David Hamilton, has written a fascinating book titled *Why Kindness is Good for You*. In it, he suggests – although it may not always feel like it – that offering love and kindness isn't just good for the people receiving it, but also for ourselves. He shares remarkable research from international universities, showing that acts of kindness are almost more important for the person carrying them out. They allow the body to produce the hormone oxytocin, which helps with a number of brain functions and keeps us happier and healthier.

Of course, in Reiki, the Connection Symbol represents love and oneness. It has an interesting design: Five different words (Kanji in Japanese) are put into a sequence and written in a way that the end of one forms the beginning of the next. You can read it in its entirety, but the Kanji don't make sense if you separate them. Something's missing. By listening to our heart, we start piecing the puzzle back together.

As humans, we're made of a similar structure: We're designed for **social interaction, for community and love.** The body, our individual shell, can sometimes persuade us that we're individual entities, but quantum physics tells us we're not. On a deeper level, we're ALL connected. Therefore, **kindness and love** are just expressions of **who we really are.** Of our soul.

Kindness Exercise

Today, there's only one exercise, but repeated 10 times in different ways.

I'd like to challenge you to do **10 ACTS OF KINDNESS**.

Before you do the first, take a moment to sense inside and make a note (mental or written) of how you feel.

Then start your day by gathering a few ideas of how you could go out of your way to do an act of kindness to somebody. You may want to connect to Reiki and ask for guidance. Not all have to be pre-planned, though.

Here are some suggestions to start with:

- Smile at a stranger
- Check how your neighbour's getting on during these difficult times
- Call a friend you haven't spoken to in a long time
- Surprise a friend or partner with a present

- Make a donation to a charity
- Offer a kind word to the cashier at the supermarket, or the people stacking shelves/the security guard
- Do the dishes for someone else
- Finish the minor repairs everyone in your household has been waiting for
- Pick up the rubbish in the street
- Spend some quality time with a loved-one.

You might do all the above anyway...if so, choose something that's a bit more challenging for you.

It doesn't matter how big or small – just do what you feel would make *another* person happy. It may mean going out of your way, being different from how you'd usually act.

Please write a list of your acts of kindness as you go along.

At the end of the day, read the list and take a moment again to sense how you feel inside.

Then connect to Reiki, say "thank you", and *feel* the gratitude.

Application 4

CREATIVITY

We're not just individual beings created by the universe – we also have the original creative force within us. We're creators! We just need to tap into this.

Are you an artist? Or, would you like to create a piece of art for the first time?

Have you pondered about new ideas, new recipes, or wanted to write?

In a way, we're constantly creating with everything we do. We create the reality we experience. But we're often in awe of people who create *art*...even though we're all able to do this, too.

Once we tap into this intuitive power, we start to realise that creativity isn't just fun and majorly fulfilling, it also inspires us to *create change*.

And everything we do – as well as how we do it – can be a beautiful inspiration to others.

Creativity Exercise

Use your talents

1. Think of an idea you've had for a long time. To write something; to develop an idea further; to draw or paint; to create a new recipe; to sew; do handicrafts; or to re-arrange your home.

2. OR, alternatively, connect to Reiki and ask for inspiration: "Universe, what do you want me to create now?"

3. Then connect or re-connect to Reiki and ask for guidance and intuition.

4. And now, CREATE! Have fun! Be excited! Go further than you've ever done before! Really dip into it. Give yourself some time to explore your creative power. Feel the flow. Make the most of your talents.

5. When you've finished, take a moment to feel your connection with the universe and realise what you've created has only been possible because of this awesome inspiration from above.

6. Place your hands in Gassho and thank Reiki.

Application 5

JEALOUSY

Of course, *others* are creative, too! And, sometimes, they might be better at it than we are.

We can either accept this – and focus on our own talents – or we become competitive. And again, if this inspires us to develop even more amazing ideas, or gives what we're working on that extra something that makes it so unique, this is absolutely fine. But it can also turn into an emotion that's unhelpful: *Jealousy.*

To start with, let me reassure you that jealousy is an emotion as normal as anger and worry. Please don't put yourself down for it. Instead, let's look at how life could be without it...just as it's happier with less anger and worry.

Jealousy, too, has different facets: We may be jealous if our partner is cheating – or if somebody else has something we'd love to have as well. This exercise is about the latter...

Over the past chapter, we've looked at our individual talents, and the fact that we all have a unique blend of them. We can either see this as a bad thing – and be unhappy – or be amazed at the number of spirits in bodies who've all been given a different toolbox for their experiences.

If we have something – either an achievement or something material that we own – we tend to be proud of it. Not proud in the negative sense of feeling superior, but in terms of feeling happy.

If somebody *else* has something we're either unable to achieve – or worse, have the ability to achieve but still haven't – we often experience varying degrees of jealousy.

When I became bankrupt, I was seriously jealous of everybody who was still in business. Why did I have to fail, and they were thriving? Of course, without this difficult patch, I would've had no incentive to explore other avenues... and I sincerely doubt I would've been open to Reiki.

We often simply don't know whether what we're longing for really is right for us. But, rather than trying to convince ourselves it wouldn't have been right for us anyway (and who knows, maybe we'll understand it later - or receive something even better), let's apply the tools of kindness, love, and oneness. And do something that's nothing but *extraordinary*.

Jealousy Exercise

1. Feel the happiness

1. Take a moment of **deep honesty** and sense inside. Who are you jealous of? You may be surprised – it may even be an experience from your childhood. If

it's more than one person, repeat this exercise for each one.

2. Now **connect to Reiki** and ask that it help you.

3. Use the Connection symbol – or simply your intention – **and connect with the other person.**

4. Now, become aware of their joy and happiness – **and join them**. Be truly happy for them! Try to see everything from THEIR perspective.

5. Then, ask Reiki to help you accept that the universe is about abundance rather than scarcity, and ask that it **also** give *you* the joy, happiness, and achievements you're looking for.

6. Place your hands on your heart chakra and **feel the love and power of the universe**. Let Reiki flow for as long as you need.

7. To finish, place your hands in Gassho, and **thank Reiki.**

2. Let Reiki help you

In the future, you may find that the simple technique of "Emergency Reiki" can help when you feel jealousy developing inside. Be happy for the other person and give it to the universe to handle how things will turn out for yourself.

Application 6

SEXUALITY

Many topics could have been included in this program, especially in the section Application. But my guides made clear that the examples already provided are enough to provide the underlying principle – and to lead to the change we're looking for.

I was, therefore, surprised when they insisted on including one final topic, *sexuality*.

After all, it's the one topic not normally covered (or even mentioned) in spiritual books. It's something we really want to keep to ourselves. And understandably so. But...we can't ignore it completely, because it also involves other people – as well as our own sanity.

When it comes to sexuality, there's something remarkably twisted in our thinking: Why do we use descriptions of sexual activity as swear words? What do we, consciously or subconsciously, connect with sexuality? Being dirty? Using body parts that are also designed to be used on a toilet? Engaging in something only acceptable to create offspring?

One of the founding fathers of psychotherapy, Sigmund Freud, was once famously asked whether he really thought that all psychological problems are related to sexuality. He simply answered yes. Even if we don't entirely agree with this, the fact that there's often a huge degree of shame attached to sex is obvious.

This doesn't mean we can't keep a healthy degree of privacy around our sexuality. But we need to look at our conscious and subconscious views, and make sure they're helpful rather than holding us back. Only if we're aligned with our entire life can we become a truly integrated person.

Sexuality Exercise

1. Take a moment to read through the following questions and allow yourself to come up with honest answers.

    1. Am I comfortable with my sexual orientation?

    2. Am I comfortable with my sexual habits?

    3. Do I connect sexuality with love and oneness?

    4. How respectful am I about my partner's needs?

    5. In a relationship, do I talk about whether our sex life is enjoyable for both?

    6. Am I afraid of my own sexual desires? If so, can those desires be fulfilled respectfully?

2. If anything comes up that you're uncomfortable with, ask Reiki to help you deal with this: Either use the Reiji-Ho method (below) and ask what you should change – or just connect to Reiki, placing your hands on your heart, and let Reiki help to bring change.

3. Place your hands in Gassho, connect to Reiki, and ask: "Is there anything I need to change with regards to my sexuality?" Then bring your hands up to your third-eye and see if anything comes into your mind. Then place your hands on your heart and let Reiki help you to let this register. Finish by thanking Reiki.

Application 7

SPIRITUAL ROUTINE

For lasting change, nothing can replace regularity...otherwise, the daily grind will pull us back all too quickly. In addition to re-visiting the exercises you've found the most demanding, I'd strongly recommend creating a framework for a daily morning routine.

Do you start each day with a Reiki self-treatment? If not, this should be the first step: Please do! Fifteen, 20, or 30 minutes of Reiki in the morning can make all the difference. As soon as you wake up, connect to Reiki, and place your hands either in a set sequence of positions, or just follow your intuition. I've done this since my very first Reiki course and I'm certain that it was this simple routine that kept me on track.

But with the variety of experiences you'll most likely have had when working through this book, you may want to add bits and build up your personalised *daily happiness ritual*.

And don't worry – a ritual only provides a framework. The experiences will just be as unexpected, different, and exciting every time you follow it!

Create Your Daily Routine

Please take a piece of paper, connect to Reiki, ask for guidance, and **write down your own ritual**, created from your favourite exercises from this book.

Here are some suggestions (but, of course, you might have had some ideas while doing the exercises):

1. Reiki self-treatment.

2. Write down three things you're grateful for, and feel the gratitude.

3. Think of your goal for the day (to complete a task, be more patient, learn something new, understand something more deeply, undertake a certain action), then connect to Reiki and ask for help achieving it.

4. Be sure to carry out three acts of kindness over the course of the day, which you wouldn't normally do.

5. Do some physical exercise (stretching, yoga, etc.).

6. Repeat the Reiki Principles (Just for today…Do not be angry, Do not worry, Be grateful, Work with diligence, Be kind to others).

7. Add, "May Reiki guide me and protect me throughout the day" (which is what I always say to myself).

8. Ignite your "three diamonds": Connect to Reiki and feel it in your lower Tanden (navel chakra), then middle Tanden (heart chakra), and upper Tanden (third eye).

9. Use Hatsurei-Ho or a simpler version of the deep abdominal breathing with Reiki.

10. Say hello to your guide or the spirit world.

11. Repeat, "I am a spirit in a body" and/or "I am love".

12. You may want to add one special Reiki technique each day (focussing on a specific Tanden point, repeating a Kotodama, or using intuitive techniques, for example).

And now, make **today the first day** you try the ritual out. It can always be adjusted and updated over time...

Just make sure that you connect *every day*.

Application 8

MY ROLE IN THE WORLD

The framework for your *inner revolution* is set. It's now time to transition to the *outer revolution*...

We've gone from **Realisation** (we're a spirit in a body), to **Change** (how this realisation changes our awareness and perception), to **Application** (first in our daily lives, then further afield to our family, workplace, and the environment).

It's been a lot of work, and the seeds that have been planted will continue to grow.

But now, we're shifting our focus a bit. Well...a lot, actually!

Looking at the state of this planet, both of humankind and the earth itself, it's obvious that major change is needed.

Environmentally, politically, socially, spiritually – very little is as it should, or indeed *could* be.

What if *we're* meant to make these changes?

What if one of the reasons for incarnating at this time was to play our part in global change?

What would we do? What role could we have?

Going into politics? Or at least, casting our votes? Campaigning for the environment? Or, minimally, being conscious of our impact on the planet? Could we create art that makes a change? Engage in education? Help the elderly? Offer Reiki to as many people as possible?

Would we join a charity? Or establish a new one? Take a new job that has a positive impact on the world? Or simply adjust what we're currently doing?

If we could make the world a better place, how would we feel IF WE REALLY DID IT?

We're a spirit in a body – and now we're aware of it.

Do we really think we might not have a mission?

Mission Exercise

1. Connect to Reiki and **ask for guidance and clarity.**

2. Then place your hands in Gassho, ask, **"What's MY ROLE in making the world a better place?",** and slowly move your hands up to your third eye.

3. Stay there and see what comes into your mind.

   Is there one element you could change or improve? Or do you feel you might need to change direction in a drastic way?

4. Now **ask Reiki to help you with this,** and place your hands on your heart chakra. **Feel change resounding in the seat of your soul...**

   What just came to your mind may be nothing less than **fulfilling your destiny!**

5. Finish by thanking Reiki, and let the ideas develop over the course of the day.

   It might become quite a journey...

   Which now takes us to the outer revolution.

Part 3

THE OUTER
REVOLUTION

The third part of this book isn't complete... because we need to create it together. By applying the principles we've previously internalised, and acting and "re-acting" from love rather than fear, we set the outer revolution in motion.

The Outer Revolution has a simple goal: To create *community* on a personal, professional, local, national, and global level. The first topics will set the scene, and I will give a short overview plus some exercises. Many of these exercises can be adapted to work with every person, group, or situation we encounter.

In the end, it all comes down to using our altered awareness in any given situation. Indeed, the exercises from Part 2 – on realisation, change, and application – can be applied on a global scale: Just imagine the Security Council of the United Nations convening – and before they enter a discussion, they do some of the exercises!

Each member starts by connecting to their soul, and from this place engages with others: Speaking, thinking, interacting from the heart. If they disagree on a topic, they can use the exercise to look from a higher perspective and view it with the help of Reiki-guided intuition.

If their arguments clash, they could use the exercise to connect with the other person – or party, culture or nation – and ask Reiki to help them understand the other's perspective.

They could focus their efforts on finding a solution that's best for a global society of individual, incarnated souls.

The World 1

FAMILY

To start with "the outer world", we need to look at the smallest collective: The family.

Some people were born into amazing families. They're loving, supportive, and have a truly close bond.

Others struggle severely. They wonder how on earth they ended up with such a family. They may even have endured ignorance or abuse, and can't wait to get away from it.

And many had both good and difficult times, feeling closely connected to some family members and struggling with others.

But all have something in common: *We're born into a family for a reason!* Either to learn and have certain experiences – or there are karmic connections.

When we move out and eventually create our own family, both types of experiences continue.

Therefore, this exercise is meant for both the family created and expanded throughout your life, as well as your birth family. I'd suggest starting with the first and then moving on from there – either on the same day or at a later stage.

If we want to make the world a better place, we need to start with the circle of people closest to us...

Family Exercise

1. Understand

We'll start with the technique of Reiji-Ho – being *Guided by Spirit*:

1. Bring your hands together in Gassho in front of your heart and connect to Reiki.

2. Ask the universe, **"Why was I born into this particular family?"**

3. Then, slowly bring your hands up to your third eye and listen to the answers.

4. Bring your hands back to your heart chakra and thank Reiki.

2. Change

We'll also use Reiji-Ho for this one...it's an absolutely amazing exercise:

1. Bring your hands together in Gassho in front of your heart and connect to Reiki.

2. Ask the universe, **"What can I do to bring positive change into my family?"**

3. Then, slowly bring your hands up to your third eye and, again, listen to the answers.

4. Bring your hands back to your heart chakra and thank Reiki.

You could also try applying the exercises in "Living from the heart" here (page 178)

3. Help

If you've had traumatic experiences related to members of your family, please try the following techniques:

1. **Connect and understand** (page 176)

2. **Forgive** (page 150)

3. **Accept** (page 153)

4. Use **Emergency Reiki** if the memories are difficult to handle.

The World 2

WORKPLACE

There's been much talk about a **better work-life balance** in recent years, and it's absolutely vital that we improve this.

But...there's a problem: If you have a full-time or even a demanding part-time job, a good work-life balance is all but unachievable. What we need to do instead is to **make our work more enjoyable**.

After all, if you deduct the time when you're asleep, most people spend more time at work than at home. It's essential therefore, for our equilibrium, to have a **positive experience** when we're at work. Let Reiki help you with this...

If you're self-employed, please adapt this exercise accordingly; if you're retired or looking for a job, just replace the word "job" with the environment you spend a lot of time in (e.g., volunteer work, a hobby that includes others, or a school or other learning environment).

Workplace Exercise

1. Become the change you want to see

1. Bring your hands together in Gassho in front of your heart and connect to Reiki.

2. Ask the universe, **"What can I do to create a better work environment?"**

3. Then, slowly bring your hands up to your third eye and listen to the answers.

4. Bring your hands back to your heart chakra and thank Reiki.

2. A daily routine

1. Start your day at work by bringing your hands together in Gassho in front of your heart and connecting to Reiki.

2. Ask the universe, **"How can I bring positive change today?"**

3. Then, slowly bring your hands up to your third eye and listen to your **daily task**.

4. Bring your hands back to your heart chakra and thank Reiki.

Day by day, your workplace will change. And your colleagues will notice the change and enjoy their time at work more, too.

Once again, the exercises in "Living from the heart" can also be applied (page 178)

3. Challenges

If you particularly struggle with a certain colleague, please try the following techniques:

1. **Connect and understand** (page 176)
2. **Forgive** (page 150)
3. **Accept** (page 153)

4. The job itself

And finally, if you struggle with **the actual demands of your job**, rather than with the work environment, quickly connect to Reiki before you begin your work and ask the universe for help. You might be surprised...

If you find any of the above difficult, perhaps because you feel **your job is the completely wrong one for you**, then ask Reiki to help you find a better one. Just connect to Reiki, ask for help, and let the universe do the rest.

The World 3
SOCIETY

We've now arrived at an even larger scale: *Society*. Which, in fact, is just another word for "souls living together". But does society really feel like this? Do we see it as this? Is it organised as such?

I have a dream that one day this nation will rise up and live out the true meaning of its creed: We hold these truths to be self-evident, that all men [people] are created equal.

With these amazing words, Martin Luther King Jr. changed the world.

And we can complete this vision together, one small step at a time.

Society Exercise

I'd like to invite you to create your own dream, and **dream up a better world**. A world that is faithful to our essence:

1. A better society

1. Bring your hands together in Gassho in front of your heart and connect to Reiki.

2. Ask the universe, **"What could a better society look like?"**

3. Then, slowly bring your hands up to your third eye and listen to the answers. Really take your time, explore the images, ideas, and your intuition.

4. Bring your hands back to your heart chakra and thank Reiki.

2. A better economy

As the next step, let's look at the economic system and whether it serves everyone...

1. Again, bring your hands together in Gassho in front of your heart and connect to Reiki.

2. Ask the universe, **"What kind of economic and financial system would be good for the world?"**

3. Then, slowly bring your hands up to your third eye again, and explore any ideas and images you receive. It doesn't matter whether it feels like intuition or fantasy – take your time to listen.

4. Bring your hands back to your heart chakra and thank Reiki.

3. A better world

1. Bring your hands together in Gassho in front of your heart once more and connect to Reiki.

2. Now ask the universe, **"How could nations build bridges if they understood each other as groups of spirits?"**

3. Then, slowly bring your hands up to your third eye and, again, explore the ideas and images. Don't be shy – you could come up with a completely new world order.

4. Bring your hands back to your heart chakra and thank Reiki.

Now take a moment and listen inside to see how you feel about these ideas.

The World 4

ENVIRONMENT

Now – in spite of appearances – we've arrived not at a societal - or even global-level topic, but rather at our individual, as well as our collective, responsibility.

In several exercises, we looked at the amazing results of Reiki experiments with water, and how much Reiki was needed to improve it.

London tap water looks rather scary under the microscope – indicating the remarkably low quality of what's certified as safe drinking water.

Water from a natural source is clean – unless it's tampered with. And of course, this tampering is indicative of the way the world treats natural resources.

And I'm sure we can all agree that this applies to pretty much every part of nature. Pollution, chemicals, over-farming, deforestation, waste, and everyday carelessness threaten not only nature but the very survival of humankind on this planet.

The effects of Reiki on water reveal how much change is needed – and is, indeed, long overdue.

Many experiments with Reiki have shown it has amazing effects on plants. But it can also inspire us to change our own behaviour along the way.

Nature Exercise

There are a number of ways in which we, as individuals, can effect change:

1. Connect with nature

1. If you can, please spend some time outside today. Take a walk in open nature or in a park.

2. Take your time to look at the trees and plants – really feel the connection.

3. Listen to the birds, look at the squirrels or whatever animals grab your attention (maybe even a bee, a fly, or an ant) – and, again, feel the connection.

4. While you look at the wonders of nature, take a moment to feel gratitude.

5. You might even use Reiki and the Connection Symbol to establish a deeper connection.

2. Recycling

1. Take a moment to think. How much effort do you take to avoid waste? Is this a consideration when you shop? Do you recycle?

2. Listen inside and sense where you can improve.

3. Food

1. Now, take a moment to reflect: What kind of impact do your usual eating habits have on the environment? Is the produce local or flown in from far away? Is it organic or grown with the use of pesticides? Is it mass-produced in monocultures?

2. Bring your hands together in Gassho in front of your heart and connect to Reiki.

3. Now ask the universe, **"How could I change my eating habits, so I don't harm nature?"**

4. Then, slowly bring your hands up to your third eye and listen to your intuition.

5. Bring your hands back to your heart chakra and thank Reiki.

4. Natural resources

1. Bring your hands together in Gassho in front of your heart once more and connect to Reiki.

2. Now ask the universe, **"What can I do to save natural resources?"**

3. Then, slowly bring your hands up to your third eye and, again, listen to your intuition.

4. Bring your hands back to your heart chakra and thank Reiki.

5. Your personal task

1. Bring your hands together in Gassho in front of your heart and connect to Reiki.

2. Now ask the universe, **"What's the most important thing I need to do for the environment?"**

3. Then, slowly bring your hands up to your third eye and, again, listen to your intuition.

4. Bring your hands back to your heart chakra and thank Reiki.

6. Give Reiki to an apple

As a little reminder of the power of Reiki, I suggest taking two similar apples (or any other fruit), give Reiki to one of them, and then taste the difference.

The World 5

ANIMALS

When I visited friends in Hamburg a while ago, their son asked if I could give Reiki to his horse, as it had a problem with its ankle.

Other than occasionally feeding them an apple when I saw one in a field, my experience with horses had been rather limited – but I thought I'd give it a try.

When we arrived, I was introduced to the beautiful mare Chelsea, and stood at her side while giving her Reiki. After a few minutes, I was hit by intuition…it felt as if I had some kind of conversation with her. I felt that she was unhappy in her box and wanted to get out and run around. She missed her freedom and felt trapped.

I moved round to treat her ankle but soon felt this area was OK, and was drawn back to where I started.

After the Reiki treatment, my friends told me that because of the ankle, Chelsea hadn't been allowed to run outside for several weeks – obviously causing the emotions I'd intuited. The way she moved after the treatment showed that she was particularly relaxed.

The next day, I received a text message from the owners. They'd just visited her to treat a skin condition on her neck (in precisely the spot I'd been drawn to) – but Chelsea wasn't bothered by it anymore. It didn't even need scratching!

Of course, I'm sure many of you can tell similar stories about Reiki treatments for animals. They're not only remarkably receptive to Reiki – but we tend to be able to feel a really deep connection with them while treating them, too.

It still came as a surprise, though, when my guides told me that humans and animals are **on the same level**. They're a spirit in a body as well!

When I told my sister about this, she wasn't surprised at all. She reminded me that animals can feel pain, experience fear, and can love – so how are they different from us?

Once we really start to accept this, it has some rather momentous effects: How differently do we treat animals, knowing that they're spiritual beings? What impact does this have on our everyday life and interactions with them?

These exercises are designed to explore this from different angles.

Animal Exercises

1. Connect with an animal

1. If you have a pet, spend some "quality time" with them. If you don't have a pet, say "hello" to a dog on the street, the neighbour's cat, or, for instance, a squirrel in the park.

2. Try to feel how they're doing; use your intuition or use Reiki to feel a deeper connection with them.

3. Try to see and feel them as a spiritual being.

2. Give Reiki to an animal

1. Please give a Reiki treatment to an animal: Your pet; your neighbour's pet; or any animal you come across, including bees, ants, and spiders.

2. Feel the connection, sense what's going on for the animal.

3. Change your perspective

Take a moment and use your imagination: How would you feel if YOU were an animal? What might your experience be? What would you wish to change in the world? How would you like to be treated?

If you have time, you may want to go through different kinds of animals, sensing how they might feel.

4. Consider

At some stage today, take time to ponder over the following questions:

1. Do you often think about animal welfare?

2. Do you consider the impact on animals when you buy food or other products?

3. If you eat meat, do you consider how the animals lived?

4. Could you replace animal-derived products?

5. Your personal task

1. Bring your hands together in Gassho in front of your heart and connect to Reiki.

2. Now, ask the universe, **"What are the most important things I need to do for animals and animal welfare?"**

3. Then, slowly bring your hands up to your third eye and listen to your intuition.

4. Bring your hands back to your heart chakra and thank Reiki.

A BETTER WORLD

With the help of Reiki, we *can* change: First ourselves, then the world. The more we live from the heart, the more it will have an automatic effect on others.

The principles in this book can be applied to any aspect of living on this planet.

My YouTube show regularly features people sharing stories of how their inner change reflects in the outer world. You are warmly invited to share you experiences to inspire others! Just send me an email...

There is a way ...

to create a fairer society;
to leave nobody behind;
to have equality and respect.

There is a way ...

to find harmony between nations;
to create diversity in unity;
to have peace on the entire planet.

There is a way ...

to have a just legal system;
for politicians to act from their hearts;
for everybody to engage in society.

There is a way ...

To make the most extraordinary inventions
to improve our lives;
to live in harmony with nature;
to find fulfilment every day.

But it will not happen by itself.

Let's uncreate what we have created so far. Learn from it. And create the most wonderful, exciting, and love-filled universe ever.

We can do it.

Together.

Acknowledgements

I would like to express my most heartfelt gratitude to the amazing people who helped in taking this project further:

Petra Lange, my mum, for her unwavering love, support, and inspiration. And for challenging me when I was bouncing all my ideas off her. May she have the most amazing success with the inspirational novels she's writing. You are not just an inspiration to me but to the world!

Elke Rosenburg, my friend and psychic medium, for her encouragement and incredibly accurate channellings - many of which made it into this book.

Rupert Fawcett, my Reiki Master colleague, who does an exquisite job teaching Reiki at the ReikiScience Academy in London – and allows me the time to work on other projects.

Venetia Davis, Senior Director of Alternatives in London, for giving me the platform to give innovative talks and workshops - and launching this book.

Ryan Lavender, my videographer, media manager, and dear friend, for creating our wonderful online courses, helping to launch the Reiki Revolution YouTube show, and the amazing support with this book.

Shirley Mclellan, Reiki Master and "master" of English, for her thoughtful, sensitive and incredibly thorough editing of this book.

Yasmin Tetzlaff for the powerful design of the book cover.

And my wonderful students, both online and live, who so openly shared their Reiki experiences with me.

Further resources for Reiki training and support:

www.thereikirevolution.com

and

www.torstenalange.com

About the Author

Torsten A. Lange is the founder and director of the ReikiScience Academy in London. He has done extensive research into the history and spiritual foundations of Reiki and taught thousands of students worldwide. And, last but not least, he credits Reiki with saving his life and bringing it back on track!

After graduating in political sciences from Hamburg University, he began his career as an entrepreneur with businesses in Germany and the UK, and a wholesale operation in the USA. Due to unforeseen circumstances, when he was in his 30s his business collapsed, and he was made bankrupt, homeless, and on the verge of ending his life. This situation lasted for years – but the very same day Reiki came into his life, it took a turn for the better.

Amazed and puzzled how an "energy therapy" could bring such change, he decided to explore this further and started his journey of discovering the spirituality behind Reiki. His extensive research revealed new information about the history of Reiki in Japan and led him to finding the world's first independent scientific proof of the different vibrational levels that Reiki works on.

His previous publications are

Reiki Made Easy, Hay House, 2016

Proof of Reiki, Proof of Eternity, ReikiScience Publications, 2021

www.torstenalange.com

Printed in Great Britain
by Amazon